AF652201

CHILD LABOUR IN INDIA

CHILD LABOUR IN INDIA

By
Profulla Hazarika

AKANSHA PUBLISHING HOUSE
NEW DELHI

AKANSHA PUBLISHING HOUSE
R 37-B, Vani Vihar, Uttam Nagar
New Delhi-110059
Email: ektabooks@yahoo.com
Ph. : 56065579 / *9811582579*

Child Labour in India

© *Author*

First Edition 2004
ISBN 81–87606–54-1

All rights reserved. Including the right to translate or to reproduce this book or parts thereof except for brief quotations in critical reviews.

[The responsibility for the facts stated, conclusions reached etc. is entirely that of the Author. The publisher is not responsible for them, whatsoever.]

PRINTED IN INDIA

Published by M.P. Misra for Akansha Publishing House, New Delhi and Printed at Offset Press, Delhi.

Preface

Currently, child labour is rampant in India. Assam is not free from this menace of child labour. The practice of child labour is really a great discrimination in human rights against a section of children in a civilized society.

Child labour prsdsactice is considered as mixed bag in developing countries, more so in all Indian states, including Assam. Because, many people tsdshink that the child labour is a necessary evil in a developing country like India, while many others think that it is sa disgrace to the nation and its immediate abolition is necessary. The present study has been initiated with a view to analysing the magnitude and nature of the problem of child labour in the country and the state of Assam and suggest certain remedial means to minimise the intensity of the evil.

The University Grantsdfdf Commission (North Eastern Regional Office) sponsored this Minor Research Project (MRP) with financial assistance. I shall remain grateful to the authority of the UGC, North Eastern Regional Office for extending the help.

I am also grateful to Professor **H. Goswami** of Dibrugarh University who consented to advise me in the venture.

I am grateful to the Librarian and staff of Dibrugarh University Library, Director of Census operations, Assam, Labour Commissioner of Assam (Guwahati), ILO Office (New Delhi) and Assam Human Rights Commission (Guwahati)

I expregss my gratitude to all the field investigators whose companionship, coopeation and assistance during the field trips for this MRP cannot be forgotten. I also remain grateful to all the family members of child labour supplying households who patiently listened and answered to my quarries.

I am grateful to Dr. B.N. Ray Chaudhury, the then Joint Secretary, NERO, UGC, Guwahati, Dr. Jeuti Boruah, Director of Law Research Institute of Eastern Region (Guwahati) and Sri Jyoti Topon Boruah of Assam Human Rights Commission (Guwahati).

I am deeply indebted to my teachers Dr. J.K. Gogoi, Dr. K.C. Bora, Professors of Economics, Sri Khirod Saikia, Sri Bhubon Boruah and other faculty members of the Department of Economics of Dibrugarh University for their inspiration and valued advices in completion of the MRP.

I am thankful to Sri Arpan Boruah of Sonari College, Krishna Hazarika (Sonari), D.D. Das and Mina Moni Das (Amgurie), Profulla Sharma (Gaurisagar), Dilip Das (Sorogua), Gobind Sharma (Raichai), Monoj Kharia and Dhiren Robidas (Nohat), Abhaijyoti Bora (Demow) and many others who were directly or indirectly concerned with this MRP.

I am grateful to Principal, N.N. Chetia of Demow College for allowing me to undertake the research project, Sri M.N. Dutta, Vice-Principal of Demow College for going through a few chapters of the manuscript and suggesting some alterations. I am thankful to my colleagues and office staff of Demow College and Mrs. Mira Goswami of Dibrugarh University Campus for helping me at different stages of the work.

Grateful acknowledgements are due to all authors whose works have been consulted in preparing this Report. I should like to acknowledge the help extended by my wife Bonita, daughter Polin & son Pritom in completing the work.

I have been benefited from discussions with number of persons and writings of many scholars. I acknowledge my indebtedness to them, but the responsibility for the views presented and any other shortcomings in the report are entirely mine.

I strongly believe the Report will open up further discussions and new ideas; the actions against child labour practices will become more vigorous and effective.

Profulla Hazarika.

Contents

List of Tables

1

An Overview

As we march into 21st century demand for removal of and action against child labour is becoming stronger. For, the elimination of child labour practices has come to be identified as a global challenge. Rising revolution for basic human rights (BHR), World Declaration in 1990 and commitment of the nations to an action plan to implement the UN convention on the rights of the child (CRC), 1989 have emboldened the movement against child labour practices. International steps in preparation of human development indicators (HDI) and information technology revolution (ITR) that are sweeping the globe have demanded acceptance of UNO's international conventions and make a commitment for ending up the exploitative and inhuman child labour practices in all countries including India, as a part of the unfinished agenda of protection of human rights and human development.

The basic parameters conditioning the level of development, living standard and aptitudes of people and causing employment and exploitation of child labourers have changed. With the growing determination of the international agencies, such as, ILO, UN, UNICEF, UNDP etc. global and national actions in the 21st century, children must break the shackles of servitude and the world must see the ending of child labour practices soon despite the prevalence of perennial poverty.

So, Assam being a part of the global village and for that matter India, should not be an exception to the global agenda.

India, currently a union of 29 states including Assam and six union territories and a founder member of ILO, has accepted and implemented five (5) international conventions from 1919 till to date in her zeal to ending up the exploitative child labour practices. To this end, right from 1881 up to the beginning of the 21st century India has made over a dozen of legislations prohibiting the employment of children of 0-14 age group. But, such legislations are keeping the concerning enforcement departments in utter inactiveness and in great confusions as regards their force and scope. The most appreciated Child Labour Act, 1986 too is the carbon copy of the earlier Bare Act, 1935. For, thus far the nation did not have the courage to enact a simple, straightforward and a bold Act on the line of U.N. conventions out of the disparate child related labour laws. In fact, the nation appears to have lost political will as well as intellectual courage to prepare a policy framework to bring about human development and ensure human rights to toiling children by ending up the inhuman child labour practices.

So, in spite of sweeping global change in outlook and in action against child labour employment, the degree of child labour use and abuse remains to be rampant in this part of the country. Still it is feared, elimination of child labour will result in worsening of the conditions of child labourers, compelling them to strive in hunger and destitution by losing their existing employment - an experience and confidence unlike to the western European countries. So, this study is mooted for dissecting the crux of the child labour problem in India with a case study in Assam with the following objectives.

Objectives of the Study

(i) To examine the child labour elimination efforts and the magnitude of child labour in India and in the state of Assam for the period 1961-2001 AD;

(ii) To classify the child labourers according to their economic activities, identify the main causes of child labour and examine their working conditions on the basis of the field observation and survey data in Assam.

(iii) To find solution for elimination of child labour practices in the state and in the country as a whole.

Methodological Issues and Scope of the Study

Every child performs some amount of economic activity of varied degree and pattern inside and/or outside the household. So, it is very difficult to classify a child as child labourer only on the basis of harshness of work or hours of work done or type of work performed or taking all these together. Because of such definitional and identification problem it becomes very difficult to draw a concrete definition of child labour. However, economic activity which involves deprivation of primary and elementary education, loveliness of childhood, parental love and care, distortion of health, morality and psychology due to harshness of work may be considered as child labour. Such type of labour is viewed as very harmful for the child and the society.

So, those children in 5- 4 age group who have sacrificed their childhood, basic formal education and are toiling over for livelihood for own-self and/or family members either as wage paid, unpaid or self-employed worker have been covered under the definition of child labourers for the present study. Children of the same age group performing own household work under the care of their parents/guardians have been excluded from the child labour force as they fall in non-student and non- workers category.

Keeping such a difference in mind for this study out of 873 villages (in 1991) within the geographical area of Sivasagar district 35 sample villages surrounding five dispersed urban centres of the district have been purposefully selected. These urban centres are:

(i) Amguri, a town bordering Jorhat district and Nagaland on the west;

(ii) Nazira, Sub-divisional headquarters;

(iii) Sonari, Sub-divisional headquarters on the east;

(iv) Sivasagar town, district headquarters;

(v) NitaiDemow, a town bordering Dibrugarh district on the north-east.

In the first round of investigation, 35 villages surrounding these urban centres were identified where predominance of child labour was reported. On further investigation, it was found that 187 households among 2290 households of these 35 villages have child labour.

In the second round of investigation, data have been collected from these 187 households by filling in four sets of questionnaire in cooperation of the field assistants.

In the third round, data and facts so collected have been confirmed and rectified wherever necessary through personal visit of the researcher into the households of the child labourers. Observation has also been made, if any change is occurring to the sample households and in child labour activity.

Data, thus collected, have been tabulated categorising the child labourers according to their nature and activity into three (3) major groups, such as, wage paid, unpaid and self-employed child labourers. This categorisation conforms to the valid typology. Data in tabuler form have been analysed and interpreted according to the observations. While proceeding with the work guidance of the research supervisor has been strictly followed so as to arrive at unmistakable conclusion.

Sources of Data

Data/information regarding child labourers in the state are /is totally lacking. Decadal population censuses prior to 1991 census have not recorded the child labour data. Only 1991 Census Report of Assam contains some information regarding child labour in the state. Census Report of 2001 is still not published.

So, the main source of information is the field data collected through the survey in 35 sample villages in six revenue circles within the Sivasagar district.

Other data/information necessary for the study have/has been collected from the secondary sources, such as,

(i) ILO, New Delhi;

(ii) UNICEF, New Delhi;

(iii) Directorate of Census Operation, Assam;

(iv) Commissioner of Labour, Assam;

(v) Reports, Books, Journals, Periodicals and News papers.

A Brief Review of Existing Literature on Child Labour

The ILO and UNICEF have produced a large number of literatures on child labour at international level. A few of them have been briefed below.

The ILO in its "Child work, Poverty and Under development" (1981) has focused on determinants and consequences of child labour and conceptual difficulties of child labour. Out of its 9 (nine) chapters contributed by different authors, one chapter has been devoted to child labour in India, entitled as "The Economic Roles of Children in India: Methodological issues". The work has been jointly edited by G.Rodgers and Gay Standing.

The ILO, in another important work " Children at work" (1981) estimates that there are about 56 million child labourers in the world and most of them belong to Third world's developing countries. This piece of work considers the problem of child labour in different parts of the world. This masterpiece has been edited by Elias Mendelievich.

In "Action Against Child Labour" (2000) edited by Nelien Haspels and Michele Jankanish for ILO, the vital functions of national policies and programmes against child labour have been examined with reference to Thailand, Tanzania, Philippines, Eklavya in Bhopal, Madhya Pradesh (India), Jatio Sramik League of Bangladesh, Cheli-Beti programme of Nepal and DLG of Pakistan etc.

ILO in a bi-monthly journal *International Labour Review* (Vol. 132, 1993) deals with child labour problem in Africa and suggests that child labour occurs elsewhere under similar conditions and clearly states that poverty, failure of school system, predominance of informal sectors are the fundamental reasons of child employment. The journal deals with child labour problem of other countries in its various issues from time to time.

UNICEF's publication "Implementation Hand book for the Convention on the Rights of the Child" (1998) provides reference for the implementation of law, policy and practice to promote and protect the rights of children.

Child Work and Education (1998) is a collection of interesting findings of the case study of Latin America done by the UNICEF. In this study it has been discovered that child labour is not only a result of economic need or exploitation but also a consequence of children dropping out from schools to join in labour force due to poor quality of schooling. According to this study education system is bankrupt. Hence, it has suggested that education system should be reformed by and large.

Learning or Working? (1995) is a compilation of works on child labour and basic education by the UNICEF. In this study the situation of child labour in Ghana, Nigeria, Peru, India, the USA and Colombia has been described. The study argues necessity of compulsory education for elimination of child labour.

However, studies on child labour undertaken at national (all India) level and state level in India are not many. A few of them have been focused below.

B.M. Dinesh in his *Economic Activities of Children: Dimensions, Causes and Consequences* (1988) deals with economic contributions of children, the back-ground causes of child labour in karnataka state and suggesting policy measures on the basis of data collected from three places of Dakshina Kannada (rural) district in Karnataka. It presents a virtuous trend on the basis of data collected from two census operations in 1971 and 1981. According to him, incentives to reduce the fertility rate would bring down the incidence of child labour.

Myron Weiner, a Professor of MIT, in his exciting book *The Child and the State in India* (1991) with some dialogues on child labour, on education and a critical analysis of the compulsory education policies, wonders why the government of India has not removed the children from the labour force. By examining the situation of 19th century Europe, M. Weiner rejects the argument that for removal of child labour in India, income of the poor should rise and the employers be in need of a more skilled labour force. To him the causes of child labour in India are deep-rooted in the culture and her policies to combat child labour are designed on the basis of fundamental beliefs. He has drawn a pessimistic conclusion stating that "with illiteracy and child labour declining world wide at a faster rate than in India, India's global share of illiterates and child labourers will continue to increase".

A study team of Institute of Applied Man Power Research (IAMR), New Delhi has completed a case study in Azamgarh district, U.P on "Child Labour in Informal Sector" in 1992-93. The case study covers 644 working children of 492 households. The major findings of this study are as follows: (i) out of school population is the highest in U.P. and it is 50%, (ii) such child population is the main reservoir of child labour, (iii) most children are either self employed, wage paid or unpaid family workers, (iv) child labour is encouraged by their parents, for they look at a child as an asset. (v) nearly 25% child labourers work for more than seven hours in a day and most of the child labourers are semi-skilled, (vi) the various schemes for controlling and banning the child labour practices do not have any impact. For, due to negative attitude toward schooling, parents put their children in factories which are outside the purview of Factories Act and other legislation. In fact, child labour is not an economic problem alone, it has social and cultural dimensions too.

J.C. Kulshreshtha in *Indian Child Labour* (1994) considers the child labour problem of India as an enigmatic problem. He has attributed the causes of child labour, inter alia, to low wages of the adults, unemployment of the adult workers, lack of social security schemes for poor families, bigger family size, rural-urban migration, high rate of illiteracy, traditions and absence of compulsory education. He elaborately deals with the legal provisions extended to Indian children and confesses their futility. He apprises the roles of voluntary organisations in creating awareness about the evils of child labour and securing social justice for them.

Farida Shah in her *Scheduled Tribe Child Labour* (1996) outlines that the incidence of child labour gives a fatal blow on the human resource development (HRD) programmes. The study highlights that child labour problem is heavily seen where poverty and illiteracy is rampant and it is an economic necessity in case of tribal children. So, for elimination of child labour a proper understanding and evaluation of various aspects of the problem is very essential.

D.P. Chaudhury deals with child labour problem of all the states of the country excluding Assam in his *Child labour in India, 1951-1991*, published in 1996. Child labour issue of Assam has been excluded mainly because of non-availability of relevant statistics.

The Indian Society of Labour Economics (ISLE) has devoted a section of its conference issue of *Indian Journal of Labour Economics* (Vol. 40 No. 4, 1997) to discuss the problem of child labour in India and in certain areas and selective industries. The volume also furnishes abstracts of 55 articles on child labour contributed by scholars on child labour problem.

P.L. Mehta and S.S.Jaswal in their *Child-Labour and the Law* (1997) have studied the child labour problem of India with special reference to tea-stalls, sweet shops and dhabas in Simla town. The study shows that while surveying 55 establishments, out of 212 workers, 80 (37.73%) were found to be children of 5-14 age group and these children were carrying out different types of occupations in those establishments. The study focuses that the working conditions of such children are far from satisfactory. They are deprived of basic education, weekly holidays and required medical check up. The existence of child labour practice is opined to be going against the spirit of the decision of the Supreme Court and violative of constitutional philosophy of the country (India). To the authors, really extreme poverty is the main reason for wide prevalence of child labour.

Neera Burra, a representative of the UNDP carried out a field investigation in brass- ware factories, (U.P.), jem polishing factories (Rajasthan), lock making and glass factories (U.P.), diamond cutting factoriess (Gujarat) in India. The findings of the investigation have been compiled in "*Born to work: Child labour in India*" (1997). There, Neera Burra has documented the tragic plight of child labour which is as impressive as Meera Nair's prize winning film "Salaam Bombay" where the lives of street children in Bombay have been poignantly portrayed. The suffering working conditions, full of tortures and abuse, which stunt the physical and mental growth of working children have been identified and narrated through out the pages. The possibility and plausibility of removing child labour in various activities, role of vested interests in bringing a child born into the fold of labour force to work in factory, necessity of compulsory education and laws banning the child labour practices have also been discussed, here.

S.K. Khanna in *Children and the Human Rights* (1998) deals with rights of the child, actions taken against child labour at national and international level, child abuse, U.N. conventions protecting the children at work and U.N declaration of the rights of the child.

Y.S. Reddy's (edited) *Child Labour* (1999) contains various issues on child labour and socio-economic conditions of child labourers both in organised and unorganised sectors in India. The volume urges for immediate end to hazardous and exploitative child labour, support for education, and legal protection so that poor children may acquire the productive skills to promote their socio-economic conditions and lives.

Bimal Kumar in *Problems of Working Children* (2000) studies the problems of working children in lock making industry, Aligarh and brass ware industry of Moradabad. With a background chapter on history of child labour in India, he estimates the magnitude of child labour in the country for the 1961-1991 period. After discussing the various aspects of child labour on the basis of his case study findings, B.Kumar concludes that child labourers in lock making industry of Aligarh and brass ware industry of Moradabad are typical of their own class. Due to low contract wage the artisans /parents were forced to employ their children. U.P., according to him, is a site of high concentration of child labour and the informal segment of the industries bids most.

Kumar finds that selective ban pushes child labour from organised to semi- organised sector and then to un-organised sector, from respectable to less respectable type of work. So, he prescribes that programme should be launched to ban child labour in all occupations. Simultaneously, income-augmenting schemes should be started covering 100% parents of the working children. Only such approach would be effective for imposition of ban on child labour.

Literatures on child labour in Assam is very scanty. In 1999, Assam Human Rights Commission (AHRC) in collaboration with "Law Research Institute for Eastern Region" Gauhati, and Women's Studies Centre, Gauhati University has done two studies on child labour in the state.

One of them is a pilot study on "*Child Labour in Gauhati City*". This study analyses the child labour problem categorising the destitute children into three types, such as,

(i) working children,
(ii) rag-pickers and
(iii) child beggers.

The main basis of such classification is their sociological background. The study has not covered paid & unpaid domestic child labourers and the self-employed children which are most common and form the vast majority of the child labour force in the state.

The second study is à project work on "*Situational Analysis of Girl Child in Assam*". This study confines its scope and area of study into Guwahati city alone.

So, a ground level study of child labour problem of the state (Assam) has become most urgent to fill the literature and information gap and to suggest and adopt necessary measures to curb down the child labour practices in the state, for that matters in the country.

Plan of Study

Whereas the technique of the present study is of action research type, various issues relevant to the child labour problem of the state (Assam) have been discussed step-wise chapterising them as follows:

Chapter 1: Overview

The first chapter deals with change in global outlook towards elimination of child labour, objectives of the research project, methodological issues, scope and limitations of the study, sources of data, review of a few literatures on child labour and plan of study.

Chapter 2: Child labour in India - Its History and Magnitude

Under this chapter the child labour practices in the country (India) has been objectively studied from vedic period up to 2001 AD of the 21st century. It also covers estimates and magnitude of child labour in India and their state-wise distribution.

Chapter 3: Child labour in Assam - Its Magnitude and Structure

In this chapter magnitude of child labour in the state (Assam) has been estimated for the period of 1961 - 2001. Work participation of child labourers, their literacy level, age and sex structure, nature of work and gender bias and employment structure have been analysed on the basis of the findings of field study.

Chapter 4: Economics of Child Labour

Based on primary field survey data, the demand and supply pattern of child labour in Assam, work satisfaction, aspiration fulfilment, income, saving and investment pattern of the child labourers have been discussed in this Chapter.

Chapter 5: Determinants and Dynamics of Child Labour

With a brief outline of general models of determining the child labour force, the causes of child labour practices in the state, such as, economic, social, administrative and legal factors have been objectively analysed.

Chapter 6: Working Conditions of Child Labourers

This chapter has been devoted to drawing a profile of working and living conditions of child labourers in the state. Various aspects related with workings of the child labourers have been analysed on the basis of the data collected and observations made during the field trip as to reflect the realities.

Chapter 7: Abolition of Child Labour: Policy Frame work and Action Plan

This last chapter has been devoted to provide recommendations regarding policy frame work and action plan for abolition of child labour in the state.

2

Child Labour in India: Its History and Magnitude

Child labour prevailed in ancient India even before 321 B.C.[1] In most cases it was in the form of child slavery. Kautilya, during the regime of the Mauryas' (321 B.C- 185 B.C) codified some rules in a spirit of abolition of child slavery. Four important codes were as follows:

(i) Children under eight years of age were banned from carrying out low and ignoble works.

(ii) Purchase and sale of children below eight years of age was prohibited.[2]

(iii) Provisions were made to relieve oneself from slavery either paying the dues or otherwise.[3]

(iv) Wages were to be paid according to time, work and/or according to the contracts made. Wages of labourers, including the child labourers were to be settled upon before the work was actually begun.[4]

Due to sweeping socio-cultural and political changes the practice of child labour and child slavery had a declining trend during the Post-Mauryas' era. Both the institutions of child labour and child slavery were becoming less common among the Hindu society.[5]

In the Medieval period, that is during the regime of Mughal kings (1200-1700 AD) exploitative child labour practice was most prevalent. It was mainly due to (i) increasing human population pressure, (ii) recurrence of famine and (iii) the fact that the rulers did nothing for improvement of the conditions of common people and those of child labourers in particular.

Child labour in British India (1708-1947AD)

Under the patronage of the East India Company certain industrial organisations grew in the 18th and 19th centuries involving employment of large number of artisans specially in weaving, carpentry, silk etc sectors. Gradually the speed had been increasing. The new sets of establishments/organizations replaced earlier family based farm-economy and opened there in, opportunity for wage-paid employment, formation of labour unions, labour markets and a new socio-economic order. But prolonged scarcity of food and extreme poverty caused by famines, lack of education and absence of compulsion for child education up to a certain age-limit, large-scale unemployment of adult workers had resulted in introduction of children into labour market. Such grim situation unleashed lot of socio-economic problems. Amongst those, employment of children of tender ages was identified as one of the burning issues of the 18th century.

In the 19th century employment of children in jute and cotton mills, mines, factories and underground work grew without age bar, working hours and sex considerations. Lack of state regulation regarding wages, working hours, age limit and child employment resulted in limitless abuse and exploitation of workers by their employers. Child labourers had been the worst sufferers. The phenomenon drew the attention of the public leaders, philosophers and the social activists and they interacted their views with the British Company government in India. The factory workers too in the country for the first time united together in 1875 for securing better working conditions in factories and consolidated a trade union movement opposing dangerous working conditions in factories, specially for women workers and children. As a result of these developments several laws had been introduced by the British Company Government in India regulating the employment of child labour.

(a) Factories Act, 1881

In spite of active opposition from the employers, the Company government passed the first legislation in 1881 for protecting the interest of labourers, including the child labourers. It came to be known as Factories Act 1881. The salient provisions of this important Act (1881) concerning child labour are as follows:

(i) It prohibited employment of children below seven years of age in factories;

(ii) Employment of a child labourer in two separate factories on the same day was banned;

(iii) Working hours for children was limited at nine hours a day;

(iv) It made provisions for four holidays in a month, rest intervals to workers and fencing of dangerous machines for safety of the workers (including child workers).

The Factories Act (1881) had to be modified several times till 1948 on the basis of the recommendations made by the Factory Commission 1884, the Freer Smith Committee 1906, the Factory Labour Commission 1907 and the Royal Commission on Labour 1929-1931.[6]

The major amendments affecting child labour incorporated in the Factories Act, (1881) till 1947 were as such-

(i) By its amendment in 1922, the minimum age for employment of a child in factories was raised to 12 years in order to give effect to the ILO (1919) conventions.

(ii) Under the modified Factories Act (1922) a child was defined as a person who has not completed 15 years of age.

(iii) By its 1911 and 1922 amendments an employer was required to submit age and fitness certificate of the child labourers employed in her/his factories.

(iv) By the amendment in 1923, working of children at night was banned and employment of women below 18 years of age in certain process works was also prohibited.

(v) By its amendments in 1926 and 1931 certain penalties were imposed on parents and guardians for allowing their children to work in two separate factories on the same day.

(vi) Under the amendment of the Factories Act, 1934, the maximum working hours for a child labourer in the age group of 12-15 years were fixed at five hours in a day. The Act was further amended in 1935, 1936, 1940, 1941, 1944, 1945, 1946, and 1947. In the post- independence period this Act was again amended in 1948.

(b) Mines Act, 1901

The second major legal provision for protecting the child labourers was the passing of the Mines Act, in 1901. The Mines Act. (1901) prohibited employment of children in mines below 12 years of age. This Act was passed, because in 1901 in 1800 mines in different parts of the country out of 200,000 workers over 5,000 children were found working in most dangerous conditions.

The subsequent amendments to the Mines Act (1901) brought about following improvements -

(i) The Mines Act was first amended in 1923. Under this amendment the minimum age for employment of a child in a mine was raised from 12 to 14 years.

(ii) The working hours was fixed at 60 and 54 hours a week for the over ground and the underground child workers, respectively.

(iii) The working days were limited to six a week.

(iv) Another amendment to this Act was made in 1925 in order to improve the working conditions of the labourers and the safety in the mines. The other amendments of the Mines Act were made in 1928, 1929, 1935, 1936, 1937 and after independence in 1952.

(v) Through its amendment in 1935, the age of child labourer in mines was further raised to 15 years. The concept of "young person" was introduced and such young persons were allowed to work having usual physical fitness certificate. [7]

(c) Indian Ports Act, 1908

The third major legal provision was the passing of the Indian Ports and Docks Act, 1908. A series of legislations relating to docks and ports prohibiting employment of children had been passed since 1889. But a consolidated Act was brought in to operation in 1908. By an amendment to the Ports Act in 1922 employment of children, below the age of 12years in ships, ports and docks was prohibited. Since then a series of Acts came in to operation. Most of these Acts were amended and consolidated again by passing "The Indian Merchant Shipping Act" in 1923. By this Act of 1923 the minimum age for employment of children was raised from 12 to 14 years. The Act was amended several times after India's independence.

(d) Assam Labour Emigration Act, 1901 and the Tea District Emigrant Labour Act, 1932

The fourth major legal provision affecting the child labour, albeit marginally, was the passing of the Assam Labour Emigration Act 1901[8] and The Tea District Emigrant Labour Act 1932, which aimed at regulating the conditions of recruitment of labour for employment in the tea gardens of Assam only. Under these Acts, persons below the age of 16 years of age shall not be employed in tea gardens of Assam and should not be imported to work in the tea gardens unless they were accompanied by their parents or close relatives. [9]

(e) Children Act, 1933

The fifth major legal provision for the protection of child labour was the enactment of the Children (Pledging of Labour) Act in 1933.

The main objective of this Act (1933) was to prevent pledging of the labour of a child, make such agreements void and stop exploitation of children. Through this legislation it was also attempted to eliminate the evils arising out of pledging of the labour of young children by their parents or guardians for taking of loan or advance. The important provisions of this Bare Act are as follows:[10]

(i) Under this Act (1933) a person below the age of 15 years is treated as a child.

(ii) Penalty has been provided under the Act. up to Rs. 50/ for pledging/ making agreement to pledge the labour of a child by the parents or guardian.

(iii) The Act has provided that the opposite party or the employer of the child whose labour has been pledged is to be fined by an amount up to Rs. 200 for the breach of the law.

This Act was amended after independence.

(f) Employment of Children Act, 1938.

The sixth major legal provision protecting the child labour in the country was the passing of the Employment of Children Act in 1938. The objective of this Act is to prevent the evils of child employment in workshops and factories not covered by the Factories Act. The Act (1938) was amended in 1939 and 1942. In its first amendment in 1939 employment of children below 12 years of age was banned in 10 processes. These are:

(i) *Bidi* making,

(ii) Carpet weaving,

(iii) Cement manufacture and bagging of cement,

(iv) Cloth printing, dyeing and weaving,

(v) Manufacture of matches, explosives and fire works,

(vi) Mica-cutting and splitting,

(vii) Shellac manufacture,

(viii) Soap manufacture,

(ix) Tanning and

(x) Wool cleaning.[11]

In spite of such important legislations, the child labour laws regulating and prohibiting the employment of children in various economic activities and sectors, failed to achieve their cherished goals. For, though the volume of child labourers in the registered factories had constantly been falling from 5.9% of the total labour force in the factories in 1892 to 0.48% in 1948 in the country, the evils of child labour continued to stay. According to Labour Investigation Committee Report (1946) the main reasons of it, inter alia, was the inadequate machineries, inspecting staff and their inefficiency to ensure the implementation of the provisions of the laws.[12]

Secondly, a large number of unregulated factories and the informal sectors did not come under the purview of the Factories Act of the country or others.

Thirdly, equally important is withering away of traditional livelihood of people and poverty. The employment of children for wages to supplement family income has become imperative for a poor family.

Child Labour in Post-Independent India

No change was observed in the child labour scenario of India immediately after independence. In 1948 on an average, daily over 11,444 child labourers were found working in different factories in the country.[13] Having been not satisfied with the efforts put by the British government for regulating the employment of child labour, the government of India has further introduced several steps for regulating the child labour employment. The history of efforts put by the government of India in post-independence period can be divided into two phases; from 1947 to 1980 and from 1980 onward.

The First Phase

A. In the first phase several legislations were enacted for improving the conditions of child labourers. These are as follows:

(a) Amendment to The Factories Act, (1948)

The earlier Factories Act was amended in 1948, after India's independence to bring about certain changes. Under the new Act of 1948, a child has been defined as a person who has not completed 15 years of age. The minimum age for employment in factories has been raised to 14 years. Non-adult workers, if they are required to work, must have physical fitness certificate with the employer of them. Otherwise, such child workers must bear a token giving reference to the certificate of fitness.

Even with the latest amendment to the Factories Act, in 1987, the Indian Factories Act, 1881 has not undergone any substantial change in its character.

(b) The Minimum Wages Act, (1948)

This Act of 1948 is a landmark in the history of child labour legislation in the country. For, it recognised that wages cannot be left to be determined entirely by the market forces. The wages of the children belonging to 14-18 years age group working in various sectors/activity came to be regulated by the Minimum Wages Act, 1948. The Act empowered the Union and the State governments to fix minimum rate of wages payable to the employees, including the child labourers.[14]

(c) Amendment to the Employment of Children Act, (1938)

The Employment of Children Act, 1938 was amended in 1949 introducing a few new provisions in it. The amended provisions are:

(i) The minimum age for employment in workshops was raised from 12 to 15 years.

(ii) The Act also prevented the employment of children below 15 years of age in hazardous and unhealthy occupations, in occupations connected with transport of passengers and goods by railway and/or port authority.[15]

(iii) Children between 15-17 years of age had been permitted to work/employed, if they were allowed 12 hours rest at night and in case of railways and ports their authorities had to maintain a Register showing their names, rest intervals and date of birth of the children employed.[16]

(iv) The Labour inspector was empowered to refer the matter to the prescribed medical authority for verification of age in case of dispute arising between the employer and the Labour inspector.

(v) The provisions of the Act were extended to cover all the factories employing young persons but not covered by the Factories Act.

(d) The Plantation Labour Act, (1951)

The Plantation Labour Act 1951 was passed preventing the employment of children under 12 years of age in plantation works such as, in Tea, Coffee, Rubber and Cincona throughout the country, except in Jammu and Kashmir. Its implementation was delayed till 1954 due to slump in plantations in the country. This Act was amended in 1960. After the repeal of the Tea District Emigration Act (1932) in 1970, the scope of the Plantation Labour Act was broadened. This was facilitated by amending the Plantation Labour Act in 1981.

(e) Amendment to the Mines Act, (1952)

The original Mines Act (1923) was further amended after India's independence, in the years of 1952 and 1984. This elaborative Act in its latest amendment has raised the age limit for employment of children in mines from 15 to 18 years. The new Act permits employment of a child in underground works, if she/ he fulfills two main conditions-

One, the child must have completed 18 years of its age.;

Two, the child must have a certificate of physical fitness from a medical surgeon.

In spite of that the Act (1984 amendment) has been found inconsistent in its provisions for it permits employment of "adolescents" (15-17 years children) in underground works in mines.

(f) The Merchant of Shipping Act, 1958.

The original Indian Shipping Act (1923) was repealed to enact a new Law in 1958. Under the new Act, 1958 employment of children below 15 years of age in general and below 18 years in particular as trimmer and stocker has been prohibited. The Act actually has come into force from 1958 onward.

(g) The Motor Transport Workers Act, (1961)

This Act was passed in 1961 protecting the employment of children below 15 years of age in Motor Transport undertakings.

(h) The Apprentice Act, (1961)

Repealing the original Act of 1850, a new apprenticeship Act was passed in 1961. This Act provides major legal provisions for protection of children, preventing putting of children below 14 years of age as apprentice for undergoing apprenticeship training in any trade, commercial, industrial, private or government establishment.

Secondly, the new Act provides severe penalties with imprisonment up to six months, or with fine up to Rs. 500/ or with both for violating the provisions of the Act.

But, the Act has been found to be self-defeating for it permits apprenticeship training under section-4, if guardians/parents of the children enter into a contract for apprenticeship with the employer.

(i) Bidi and Cigar workers Act, (1966)

To protect the interest of the children employed in *Bidi* industries, the govt. of India passed the *Bidi* and Cigar Workers (Conditions of employed) Act, in 1966. This Act, like any other Acts, contains provisions in regard to regulation of contract system of work, hours of work, rest interval, annual leave with wages, working conditions and prohibits employment of children below 14 years of age. In addition, night works by the children in 14-18 age group has been prohibited in case of certain industries.

(j) Shops and Establishment Acts.

Passing of the Shops and Establishment Acts during post-independence period, by the state governments for their respective states are the major legal provisions protecting the children employed in commercial establishments, hotels, dhabas etc. These Acts have empowered the state governments to vary the minimum age and extend the coverage of the Acts in establishments other than shops and commercial establishments.

Accordingly, the minimum age for employment in such establishments has been fixed at 12 years in Bihar, Goa, Daman and Diu, Gujrat, J&K, Karnataka, M.P., Manipur, Orissa, U.P, Rajasthan, Tripura and West Bengal; at 14 years in Andhrapradesh, Assam, Chandigarh, Delhi, Hariyana, Himachal-Pradesh, Kerala, Meghalaya, Pondicherry, Panjab and Tamilnadu.

In Maharastra, the minimum age of employment in shops and commercial units is 15 years. There is no separate shops and commercial establishments Act in Andaman and Necobar, Arunachal Pradesh, Dadra and Nagar Haveli, Laksha deep, Nagaland and Sikkim.[17]

In Assam, The Assam Shops and Establishments Act has been passed in 1971 but it has come into operation from 1974 regulating the employment of children employed in shops, commercial establishments, and establishments for public entertainment and/ or amusement in the state.[18]

(k) The Contract Labour Act, (1970)

Another major legal provision provided in the Post-independence era, for the protection of the children is the passing of the Contract Labour (Regulation and Abolition) Act in 1970.

The 'contract labour' employed in industries, mines, plantations and docks etc. is different from the 'bonded labour'. The contract labourers are not directly recruited by the establishments, their names do not appear in the pay roll and they are not directly paid by the employer.

The National Commission on Labour, 1969 observed persistence of child labour in various unorganized sectors and establishments in varying degrees. Following such report, this all India Act was passed in 1970, which covers all establishments and contractors employing 20 or more workers.

Whereas no specific provision was made in this Contract Labour Act (1970) prohibiting child employment, so child labour had been observed in building works, construction of roads and in certain other establishments under the contractors. Thus, the main objective of the Act had failed though the system of contract labour was abolished in the country by the passing of the Act in 1970.

B. Another major development in this phase was the granting of Constitutional Safeguard to the children.

In 1950, the constitution of independent India came into force, and laid down special provisions for the protection of children against any discrimination on the ground of religion, race and/or caste.[19]

Under the Constitution protection of children against any form of exploitation had been considered as their fundamental rights.[20] So, employment of a child below 14 years of age in any factory, mine and/or in hazardous work was banned.

In addition, under the directive principles of the Constitution, state governments were made obliged to prepare policies for healthy development of children in conditions of freedom and dignity so that their childhood and youth are well protected against abuse and/or exploitation, moral and material abandonment. Providing of free and compulsory education to children till their completed age of 14 years, thus, become the commitment of each state.[21]

C. The government of India to assess the position of child labour had appointed a Committee Headed by Gurupad Swamy.

This committee on child labour in its reports submitted in 1979 made the following observations:

(i) India is one of the countries in Asia where a largest majority of children are working;

(ii) Child labour problem in India is openly manifested;

(iii) Child labour in the country becomes an absolute evil;

(iv) A child labourer in India is required to work beyond her/his physical capacity, and longer hours which is interfered by her/his tender age; and

(v) Wages paid to a child labourer is much lower than the quantum of works done.

In spite of such harsh reality the Ministry of Labour in India rejected an idea of child labour abolition effort. For it viewed that abolition of child labour is not an economic feasibility, but a necessary evil. Far from withdrawing children from workings, provision for training of children to labour better was organised. For example, in 1978 Hand loom and Handicrafts Exports Corporation (HHEC) at Delhi had set up training centers for children where after undergoing eight (8) hours training a day for one year, a child could enter into carpet industry or others for employment. Such retrograde policy of the government had complicated the child labour abolition task.[22]

The Second Phase

A. Sensitising the Issue of Child labour in India:

From the early 1980s several events took place, which made the child labour a national issue debated in various public fora. Two such major cross current events sensitising the issue are -

(a) Frightening Volume of Child labour Estimates:

In 1983 the Planning Commission of India estimated the child labour force in the country at 17.36 million, The Operation Research group of Boroda estimated it to be 44 million and a net-work of 700 NGOs under "Campaign Against Child Labour" estimated at 70 to 80 million. Such estimations caused much alertness among the various sections of the society.[23]

(b) Formation of NGOs for Fighting the Menace of Child labour:

The South Asia Coalition on Child Servitude (SACCS), an NGO working with government officials in India raided some sites where children are known to be working in intolerable conditions and released some 29,000 children since its inception in 1983 till 1985.[24]

The Bonded Labour Liberation Front (BLLF) another NGO working in Uttar-Pradesh exposed the phenomena of child bondage bringing the tragic plight of 32 bonded children to public notice through writ petition in the Supreme Court of India in 1984. The tragic story of the 32 children revealed and represented the facts of hundreds and thousands of them.[25]

The Anti Slavery Society of India (ASSI) reported in 1984 that there were about 100,000 children employed to work in carpet industry in conditions of slavery.[26] Most of such ill-fated children were below 12 years and kidnapped from the perennially draught prone areas of Bihar state, particularly from its Palamau district. Some were pledged by their parents for paltry sum of money, as they found no use of keeping their children with them (parents) and seeing them die in hunger. Many of such kidnapped or pledged children were kept in captivity and employed in carpet industry in Mirzapur and Bhadohi area of Uttar Pradesh. The BLLF released such children from slavery, some were returned to their native places and got many of them rehabilitated.

A Bangalore based NGO (Bangalore Oniyavora Seva Coota, 1984, known as BOSCO) initiated the debate by drafting a bill on child labour. The group argued that poverty is the main cause of child labour and so it cannot be legislated away. The NGO further believed that prohibition of child labour would be counter productive. So, attempt should be made to regulate their working conditions rather than to prohibit such works and there should be no minimum age for children to enter into the world of work.[27]

The bill got wide publicity, public response for discussion and media coverage. Considering the bill, public pressure, exposures of the NGOs and the global developments in respect of promoting the child welfare the government of India finally passed the Child Labour (Prohibition and Regulation) Act in 1986.

B. Enactment of the Child Labour Act, 1986:

For the enthusiasts the significance of the Child Labour Act, 1986 is that it has laid down the age limit, wage rate and hours of work for the child labourers employed in various activities and provides safeguards for health, safety and work conditions for such children. It was further expected that the rampant exploitative child labour practices would slow-down to its lowest ebb. The Act, 1986 has, also left such an impression that for the first time a child labour Act has been passed in the country and that child labour problem was not present ever before.

In fact the provisions of the Child labour Act, 1986 are almost identical to those in the Employment of Children Act, 1938 where employment of children below 14 years of age have been banned in certain occupations and process of industries. The same criterion of age (14 years) has been used in the Child Labour Act, as it is fixed in the Factories Act, 1948. The only difference between the laws of 1938 and 1986 is that the latter provides for constitution of a "Child Labour Technical Advisory Committee" (CLTAC) to investigate the processes in different industries in the country from time to time in order to determine whether they are hazardous or otherwise.

Keeping the plethora of child labour related laws in simultaneous operation, the Child labour Act, 1986 has practically made no meaningful contribution in regulating the child labour practices. Instead, it has rather confused the law users and given furrows for unabated employment and exploitation of poor children.

C. Adoption of National Policy on Child Labour:

Realising the fact that child labour is a social evil, which cannot be removed by simple enactment of law and left aside as the phenomena of traditions, extreme poverty, social backwardness and high level of unemployment but can be mitigated to some extent, the government of India introduced a national policy on child labour in 1987.

The national policy on child labour, 1987 provides for carrying out the legislative provisions and general development programmes for the benefit of child labourers and child labour projects. Altogether 14 national child labour projects have been set up in highly concentrated child labour areas of nine (9) states. Out of these two (2) projects have been carried out with ILO.s assistance but within the framework of national policy.

These are:

(i) International Programme on Elimination of Child Labour (IPECL) and

(ii) Child Labour Action and Support Programme (CLASP).

In addition, for tackling the child labour problem, the government of India set up a separate agency in 1994, called - "National Authority for Elimination of Child Labour (NAECL). During 1995-1996 at the behest of the NAECL in all states of the country Child Labour Cells (CLC) were created, while a few states set up Task Forces (TFs) to eliminate the child labour practices.

Besides, out of a total 362 districts in 11 states of the country, the NAECL had identified 137 districts experiencing a very high incidence of child labour and hence established District Committees in each to activate the campaign against child labour. Such District Committees have a mandatory obligation to report the progress of elimination of child labour from time to time to the NAECL of India.

The main functions entrusted to the NAECL are:

(i) to lay down policies and programmes for elimination of child labour;

(ii) to monitor the progress of implementation of projects, programmes and schemes for elimination of child labour;

(iii) to co-ordinate the various child labour related programmes implemented in the country.

D. Adoption of the Convention of the Rights of the Child. (CRC, 1989)

India made a commitment to eliminate the exploitative child

labour practices by accepting the UN,s CRC, 1989 in 1992. The United Nations' CRC 1989 is an update of the Geneva Declaration of the Rights of the Child in 1924 and the UN Declaration of the Rights of the Child in 1959.

The world summit for children in 1990 organised under the banner of the UN was attended by the representatives of the states and governments of 159 countries. These world leaders endorsed the convention of "Rights of the Child" and jointly signed a declaration in 1990 popularly known as "World Declaration" (WD) for the survival, protection and development of children and a plan of action to implement the World Declaration, 1990. India was one of the signatories of it that committed to ensure compulsory and free primary education for all children. The CRC, entered into force in 1990. It recognises the need for specific attention to protect and promote the rights of children, to support their growth and development for becoming worthy citizens of the world.[28] It also represents international commitments to entitle the childhood special care and assistance, right to live, survival and development, and protection against all forms of discrimination or punishment. The CRC, 1989 has, so far, been ratified by 191 countries including India, till 2001 A.D.

E. National Human Rights Commission (NHRC) and Child Labour

The NHRC in India came into existence in Oct. 1993 for realising the unfinished agenda of human rights and full human development in the country. However, this is being done after a long span of the UNO's Universal Declaration of Human Rights in 1948.

In addition to CRC (1989), certain other cross- currents of events, which influenced the formation of the NHRC of India, are as such-

(i) ILO has been active since its inception in 1919 in containing the exploitative child labour practices. It has set altogether 173 international conventions and 180 recommendations with respect to child labour inter alia, as regards the minimum age- limit, working hours, wage rate, conditions of employment and social security.[29]

Certain member countries of the ILO have ratified these conventions and passed legislations to limit the child labour practices. The minimum age limit of 18 years set by the ILO in 1973 has been accepted only by Libyan. It has been found that the minimum age for employment of child labour in other member countries have varied from 14 to 16 years.

India, being a member of the ILO has ratified altogether 36 conventions out of 173 till 1992 and has accepted 14 years as the minimum age limit for employment of a child.

(ii) UN declared the year of 1979 as the International Year of the Child and dedicated a whole decade to the improvement of children from neglect, destitution and deprivation. It influenced the views of Human Rights activists in the country.

(iii) Apart from a Programme of Action for Elimination of Exploitation of Child Labour (PAFEECL) adopted by the UN Commission on Human Rights in 1993, UNICEF (1946) started a campaign to eradicate the malady of child labourers in developing countries, including India.

UNICEF in its report in 1997 emphasises that end of hazardous child labour should not wait for poverty end. For, the world poverty cannot be eliminated by the end of a decade but the hazardous child labour and violation of human rights of the children can be stopped.[30]

Keeping in view all such global and local developments the NHRC of India emphasised the co-ordination between government, Judiciary, Media, Legal Professionals and the NGOs and in 1997 declared a blanket ban on Govt. servants from employing children below 14 years of age as domestic servant. The Commission further recommended for amendment of the service rules of all states accordingly, and the state governments did so. The government of India too amended the Central Services (Conduct) Rules, 1964 prohibiting employment of children below 14 years of age by the govt. servants and violation of it amounts to attracting major penalty.

Estimation of Child labour in India

In spite of over a dozen of important legislations, active role of NHRC, NGOs and international agencies such as, UN, ILO, and UNICEF, exploitative child labour practices in the country still remains to be rampant, for that matters in whole of South-East Asia (Table-2.1).

Various authorities and organizations have estimated the magnitude of child labour in India (Table- 2.2). But these figures differ widely. Whereas, Census figures are more authentic, consistent and reliable, have been used to delineate the trend of child labour in the country.

Estimates based on Census data show that the magnitude of child labour in India has increased from 133 lakh in 1951 to 136 lakh in 1981 and to 231 lakh in 1991 (Table 2.3). However, the trend was expected to decline in the country to 109 lakh child labourers in 2001 like in other regions of Asia (China and Japan) due to falling death and birth rates, change in attitude of parents as well as of the society towards child and child labour, efforts of the UN, national government, Human Rights activists and the NGOs in the country for elimination of brutal and exploitative nature of child labour practices.

Contrary to such expectations the last decade has witnessed a rapid increase in child employment in informal sectors in the country. For example, in 1999 in Bihar's Sonepur cattle fair, children have been sold for a price of Rs. 900 for each. During 1999-2000, this fair alone has supplied over 200 children to Punjab, Delhi and Hariyana.[31]

However, it is found that of the total child labour force of Asia, India shares 26.4% (and of the total population of Asia, India shares 24.1% population) in 1971, 19.9% (25.5%) in 1981, 40.6% (27.6%) in 1991 and 16.5% (29.8%) in 2001 (Table- 2.4).

Table–2.1

Economically Active Children Below 15 years of Age in the World & Sub-Regions (Figures in '000)

	Year	1980		1985		1990		Change in 1980-1990	1998	
i.	World	87,867	(100.00)	80,611	(100.00)	78,516	(100.00)	-9,351	370,110	(100.00)
ii.	Africa	14,950	(17.01)	14,536	(18.03)	16,763	(21.35)	1,813	87,200	(23.56)
iii.	America	4,122	(4.69)	4,544	(5.64)	4,723	(6.02)	601	19,080	(5.16)
									78,340	(21.17) *Other countries*
iv.	Asia	68,324	(77.76)	61,210	(75.93)	56,784	(72.32)	-11,540	204,520	(55.26)
(a)	East Asia	39,725	(45.21)	33,463	(41.51)	22,448	(28.59)	-17,277	74,300	(36.33)
(b)	South Eastern Asia	6,518	(7.42)	6,079	(7.54)	5,587	(7.12)	-931	28,940	(14.15)
(c)	Southern Asia	20,192	(22.98)	19,834	(24.60)	27,639	(35.20)	-7,447	91,840	(44.91)
(d)	Western Asia	1,880	(2.14)	1,834	(2.27)	1,109	(1.41)	-771	9,440	(4.61)

Sources: (i) D.P. Chaudhury, (1996) A Dynamic Profile of Child labour in India, 1951-1991, P.91 adopted from ILO Bulletin of Labour Statistics, 1993-Table-11, p. 91

(ii) World Bank, (2000) Entering the 21st Century, World Development Report 1999/2000.

* Figure in Brackets are the percentages

** Figures estimated from the tables furnished by the world Bank in the World Development Report 1999/2000, pp-234-235.

Table–2.2

Estimates of Child labour in India Below 15 years of Age, 1951-1991.

Organisations/ Persons and year	1951	1961	1971	1981	1991	Change over 1951-1991
			Total child workers in 0-14 age group			
(i) Census data based Estimates[(1)]	13,387,144	14,469,775	10,753,985	13,640,873	23,161,013	* (+ 9.8 Million)
(ii) NSS data based Estimates[(1)]	11,339,526	13,299,910	16,330,000	18,611,659	24,449,047	(+ 13.11 Million)
(iii) F.Shah's Estimates[(2)]	NA	14,500,000	NA	16,300,000	17,580,000	(+ 3.08 Million)
(iv) ILO's Estimates[(3)]	NA	23,985,000	25,371,000	NA	44,000,000	
(v) P.L. Mehta & S.S Jaswal's Estimates[(4)]	NA	14,469,774	10,753,982	11,168,819	NA	

* Child labour figures, excluding Assam state.

Sources: (1) D.P. Chaudhury, (1996) A Dynamic Profile of Child labour in India, 1951-1991. P.92

(2) F. Shah; (1996) Scheduled Tribe Child Labour; (Udaipur) Shiva Publishers and Distributors, P.15.

(3) ILO; (1978) Year Book of Labour Statistics.

(4) P.L. Mehta & et al; (1997) Child Labour and the Law, (New Delhi) Deep and Deep Publications, P. 16.

Table–2.3
Child Population, School going Children, Non-Workers-Non Students and Child labourers in India, 1951-2015

Year	Total Child Population (0-14)	Child Population (5-14)	School Attending Children (5-14)	Children Not Attending School (5-14)	Non-Workers Non-Student (5-14)	Child Labours (Marginal´+ Main workers) (5-14)
	Col-1	Col-2	Col-3	Col-4	Col-5	Col-6
1951	1338,80,440	866,11,750	235,24,477	630,87,273	497,00,129	133,87,144
1961	1800,82,782	1139,80,144	345,95,760	793,84,384	649,14,609	144,69,775
1971	2303,94,772	1507,78,259	505,42,151	1002,36,108	894,82,123	107,53,985
1981	2631,07,053	1795,97,245	764,15,059	1031,82,186	895,41,313	136,40,873
1991	2969,36,090	2033,00,112	829,70,793	1203,29,319	971,68,306	231,61,013
2001	3397,74,600 *(3334,06,000)	2360,69,300 (1898,25,537)	1007,86,100 (846,86,278)	1352,83,200 (1051,39,259)	1012,91,000 (941,52,343)	339,92,200 (109,86,916)*
2015	5072,56,430	2953,89,150	1272,45,200	1681,43,950	1077,15,000	604,28,950

Sources: (i) For Figures of 1951, 1961, 1971, 1981 and 1991 in cols 1, 2, 3, 4, 5 and 6, Census of India of the respective years.

(ii) Figures for 2001 and 2015 in 0-14 and 5-14 age groups in cols 1, 2, 5 and 6 have been projected with appropriate population method, based on the growth rate of child population during 1971-1991 in the respective columns.

*Figure in brackets are the projected child population in 2001 by D.P. Chaudhury in Dynamic Profile of India, (1996) Tables-1.2 and 2.1.

(iii) Child labour figures for 1991 are the 1991 Census based estimates.

Table–2.4
Population and Child labour force in Asia and India, 1971-2015

Year	Population			Child Labourers		
	in Asia	in India	% Share of India	in Asia	in India	% Share of India
1971	2265 (Million)	548 (Million)	24.19	40.453 (Million)*	10.7 (Million)	26.45
1981	2671 (Million)	683 (Million)	25.57	68.3 (Million)	13.6 (Million)	19.9
1991	3056 (Million)	846 (Million)	27.68	56.8 (Million)	23.1 (Million)	40.6
2001	3442.8 (Million)	1027 (Million)	29.83	205.0 (Million)	33.9 (Million)	16.53
2015	3797 (Million)	1211.7 (Million)	31.91	215.3 (Million)	60.4 (Million)	28.04

Sources: (i) Human Development Report, 2000.
(ii) World Development Report 1999/2000.
(iii) ILO; Year Book on Labour Statistics, (1978) Pp. 16-47.
* Figure relates to the year of 1975.

Table–2.5
State wise Distribution of Working Children According to 1971, 1981 and 1991 Census.

State/Union territories	1971 Child Worker	1981 Child Worker	1991 Child Worker (c)		
			Main Workers	Marginal	Total workers
1	2	3	4	5	6
1. Andhrapradesh	1,627,492	1,951,312	1,537,293	124,647	1,661,940
2. Assam	239,349	(b)	259,953	67,645	327,598
3. Bihar	1,059,359	1,101,764	795,444	146,801	942,245
4. Gujrat	518,061	616,913	373,027	150,558	523,585
5. Haryana	137,826	194,189	89,030	20,661	109,691
6. Himachal pradesh	71,384	99,624	30,771	25,667	56,438
7. J & K	70,489	258,437	(b)	(b)	(b)
8. Karnataka	808,719	1,131,530	818,159	158,088	976,247
9. Kerala	111,801	92,854	28,590	6,210	34,800
10. Madhya Pradesh	1,112,319	1,698,597	997,940	354,623	1,352,563
11. Maharastra	988,357	1,557,756	805,847	262,571	1,068,418

(Contd...)

12. Manipur	16,380	20,217	13,478	3,015	16,493
13. Meghalaya	30,440	44,916	30,730	3,903	34,633
14. Nagaland	13,726	16,235	16,106	370	16,476
15. Orissa	492,477	702,293	325,250	127,144	452,394
16. Punjab	232,774	216,939	132,414	10,454	142,868
17. Rajasthan	587,389	819,605	490,522	283,677	774,199
18. Sikim	15,661	8,561	5,254	344	5,598
19. Tamilnadu	713,305	975,055	523,125	55,764	578,889
20. Tripura	17,490	24,204	13,506	2,972	16,478
21. U.P	1,326,726	1,434,675	1,145,087	264,999	1,410,086
22. West Bengal	511,443	605,263	593,387	118,304	711,691
23. Andaman & Nicobar	572	1,309	758	507	1,265
24. Arunachal Pradesh	17,925	17,950	11,632	763	12,395
25. Chandigarh	1,086	1,986	1,839	31	1,870
26. Dadra & Nagar Haveli	3,102	3,615	2,677	1,739	4,416
27. Delhi	17,120	25,717	26,670	681	27,351
28. Daman & Diu	7,391	9,378	741	200	941
29. Goa	-	-	3,938	718	4,656

(Contd...)

Table 2.5 - Concld.

1	2	3	4	5	6
30. Lakshadweep	97	56	17	17	34
31. Mizoram	(a)	6,314	6,391	10,020	16,411
32. Pandicharri	3,725	3,606	2,565	115	2,680
I. Census data =	10,753,985	13,640,870	9,082,141	2,203,208	11,285,349
II. Census data based estimates =	10,753,985	13,640,873	12,669,909	10,491,110	23,161,013
III. NSS data based estimates =	16,330,000	18,611,659	13,950,225	10,498,822	24,449,047

* a. Census figures of 1971 in respect of Mizoram is included under Assam.
b. Census could not be conducted.
c. Figures for 1991 census cover workers in 5-14 age group.

India's % share of child labourers may not fall further due mainly to inefficiency of the child labour elimination projects and programmes, unabated population growth and inter-regional migration of child labourers. India being a part of second "Ecumen Area",[32] she may share 28.0% child labour (and 31.9% population) of Asia in 2015 AD. (Table-2.4).

State-wise Distribution of Child labour Force:

As revealed by the Census data of the country (Table- 2.5) in 1991 Andhra Pradesh had highest incidence of child labour. Other states experiencing burden of more than one million child labourers are U.P., M.P, and Maharastra in order. Position of Assam is found to be 12th.

Causes of Child labour Growth in India:

Variables responsible for the growth of child labour force in the current socio- economic settings of the country have been observed to be multi-dimensional. Among many others, the pace of industrialisation, profit earning motives of the employers, prolonged family poverty, lack of health care and compulsory primary education, non- implementation of child labour laws, absence of best intention to regulate the child labour practices, and above all rapid population growth have been observed to be mainly responsible. As realities have unveiled, not legislation alone but addressing the larger issues of illiteracy, family poverty and over population are the only ways to tackle the child labour problem of this country. With the increasing mobility of human population across the international borders of the country, child labour in India has become a global problem. Hence, action against it is to be global type.

Notes and References

1. Tripathi, R.S. (1985) *History of Ancient India*; Motilal Banarsidas, Delhi, p. 49.
2. Kautilya (not dated) *Artha Shastra*: Asom Prakashan Parishad, Calcutta.
3. *Ibid., op.cit., sloka* No. 21.

4. Ibid., *op.cit.*, ch. 13; also Chaudhury, R.K. (1982) *Economic History of Ancient India*: Delhi, p. 131
5. Ray Chaudhury, S.C. (1997) *Social, Cultural and Economic History of India: Medieval Age*; Surjeet Publications, Delhi, p. 65.
6. S.S. Bangalee pioneered starting labour agitation in Bombay in 1875 demanding good working conditions for workers, protesting women and child employment in factories. As a result in 1875 itself First Factory Commission was appointed and the first Factories Act. came to be passed in 1881. Such type of movement was again started in 1890 in Bombay led by N.M. Lokhande. With the introduction of electric power in the factories employees had been forced to work day and night which resulted in labour unrest and setting up of a number of Commission and Committees to settle the labour problems.
7. Vaid, K.N. (1970), *Labour Welfare in India*; Shri Ram Centre for Industrial Relations, New Delhi, pp. 49-51.
8. *Ibid.*, pp-51-53.
9. Saxena, R.C and Saxena, S.R. (1992) *Labour Problems and Social Welfare*; Prakashan Kendra, Lucknow. p. 535.
10. Bhar, B.K. (1977) *Hand Book of Labour Laws*; Academic Publishers, Calcutta, pp. 402-403.
11. The Employment of Children Act 1938, section 3 (1), Section, 3(3) and the Schedule (List of Processes).
12. Saxena, R.C. and Saxena, S.R.: (1992) *op. cit.*, pp. 363-364.
13. Kulshreshtha, J.C. (1994) *Indian Child labour*; Uppal Publishing House, New Delhi, p. 195
14. Singh, J.K. (1998) *Labour Economics: Principles, Problems and Practices*; Deep and Deep Publications, New Delhi, pp. 378-388.
15. The Employment of Children Act 1938, section 3(3).
16. 1951 Amendment to the Bare Act, 1938 to conform the ILO conventions regarding night works.
17. *The Indian Journal of Public Administration*, (1979) vol. XXV, No-3, P.933.
18. Assam Shops and Establishments Act and Rules, (Assam Act XXI of 1974). 4th edition, 1997.
19. *The Constitution of India*; Article - 23 and 39(e) and (f)
20. *Ibid.*, Article - 24
21. *Ibid.*, Article- 39 (e) and (b) and Article - 45.
22. Khanna, S.K. (1998) *Children and the Human Rights*; Commowealth Publishers, Delhi, p. 238.

23. Castle, Robert, Chaudhury, D.P. *et al.* (1997) Labour Classes, the World Trade Organisation and Child Labour in India, in *The Indian Journal of Labour Economics*; vol. 40. No-I

24. Khanna, S.K. (1998), *op. cit.*, p. 277.

25. *Ibid.*

26. Puri, Rakhat (1984) "India has 100 million Bonded Labourers." *The Hindustan Times*, Sept 30, 1984.

27. Burra, Neera, (1997) *Child Labour in India*, Oxford University Press, Delhi. p.1

28. UNDP (2000) *Human Development Report*, Oxford University Press, Delhi, p. 44.

29. Labour Bureau, Ministry of Labour, (1994) *Indian Labour Year-book, 1992*, GOI, Delhi. pp. 189-214.

30. Singh, S.P., (1997) "Child Labour: The Malady and Remedy" in *Yojana*, July, p. 21.

31. *The Assam Tribune* (2000), 29th December, Gauhati.

32.* (i) In 1998, India is found sharing 27.39% child labour force of Asia with 13% child labourers to the 431 million labour force of the country. World Bank (2000), Entering the 21st Century.

World Bank/IBRD, Oxford University press, pp. 234-235.

* (ii) Other member countries of second largest population concentration are: Bangladesh, Mynmar, Pakistan and Srilanka.

3

Child Labour in Assam: Its Magnitude and Structure

In spite of a dozen of legislations and rules thereunder and a network of government administrative machineries protecting the interests of the children, exploitative child labour practices are growing fast in the state. Most children employed in various economic activities in informal and un-organised sectors of the state have been labouring under harsh working conditions, and confronting tortures, abuse and exploitation. Such practices have not only been adversely affecting the social milieu, but also the health, psychology, morale and normal development of the working children. The practices have become so much dangerous and harmful that many of the child labourers, who would have been the progeny of future civilization, are at a risk of being miserable in their adulthood. Such practices are the gross violation of 'human rights'. Therefore the problems of child labourers in the state of Assam have currently drawn the attention of the social scientists, social activists and academics. It has been a matter of public debate in all fora.

In the traditional Assamese society taking care of and extending protection to the children was a collective responsibility of all members of a family. So, the practice of child labour was rare to find. But with the break-down of traditional joint-family system and growth of atomic family, increasing demand for family income due to changing life-style, expanding wants, continuous fall in money value and mainly due to family poverty, children began to participate in some income generating activities. However, child labour remained to be a part of family work culture and/or family labour

Till the 1970s, most of the children who formed the body of the child labour force in the state were engaged primarily in agriculture, which was of traditional type, labour intensive and self- sufficient nature. Besides, the industrial sector was backward in the state. The service and infra-structural sectors too were underdeveloped. Under such a socio-economic environment the child labour force available in rural areas had to engage themselves in resourceful rural sector of the state. Hence, most of the child labourers were of self-employed type.

The urban centres of the state had then harboured a very little quantum of child labourers. So, the problem of child labour was less sensitised and its intensity was less felt in the state till the 1970s.

But, since the 1980s, the rapid urbanisation and expansion of state's civil and police administrations have accelerated the tertiary activities in the state, with a mild expansion of secondary sector. Concomitantly, the mechanisation and commercialisation of agriculture have made large number of child labourers redundant in the agricultural sector. Burst of population growth in rural areas added a new dimension. For, over-utilisation of finite natural resources by the increasing population has destroyed the self sustaining system of the rural- environment and diverted the redundant workers towards urban centres of the state.

So, large section of such workers including child workers are appearing in state's urban centres with their involvement in the growing trade, commerce, transport, production and processing units and in service activities, such as in tea-shops, hotels, commercial establishments etc.

The poor state of primary and secondary education too in rural areas, has encouraged a large section of rural children belonging to the poor families to drop their studies and work for wages or earning money in the neighbouring urban centres for contributing to their family purse.

During the 1990s, the free-market system tends to change the distribution pattern of society's resources, pushing the weaker sections of the society to the periphery and gradually depriving them of their command over the economic resources. Such marginalised sections of the society, in the absence of any safety net to protect their economic interests against the aggressive competitive market system, are confronting a hard time, which they try to wade through by putting their young children into work in urban places. Social traditions, codes of government legislations and family status are not troubling them for doing so. Hence, the practice of exploitative child labour is growing to be rampant in the state since the last decade of the 20th century.

Estimates of Child labour in Assam

Statistics on child labour in the state were not available in the census reports prior to 1991 census. Hence, the magnitude of child labour in the state for earlier census periods had to be estimated, from various scattered information available in the respective census reports.

The total child-population in 5-14 age group can be classified into two broad categories, such as,

(i) children attending the school and

(ii) children not-attending the school.

The children (5-14) not-attending the school can further be sub-divided into two sub-categories, such as,

(i) nowhere children and

(ii) child labourers.

Data on all these sub-categories of children were available in 1991 census reports. The magnitude of child labour in the state which is shown in Table–3.1 for 1961, 1971, 1981 have been estimated by using 1991 census proportions of children not-attending school (col.4), non- workers & non-students (col.7), and

Table–3.1

Child Population, School Attending Children, Nonwhere Children and Child Labourers in Assam. 1961-2015

Year	Chil d/Pop	Child /Pop	School going Children	Children Not-Attenting School	Child Laboaurers (5-14)		Non-Worekrs & Non-Students (5-14)	
Age group	(0-14)	(5-14)	(5-14)	(5-14)	As estimated by the Author	As estimated by the Ministry of Lab. Govt. of India, 1996-97	As estimated by the Author	As estimated by the Ministry of Lab. Govt. of India, 1996-97
	Col-I	Col-2	Col-3	Col-4	Col-5	Col-6	Col-7	Col-8
1961	5,000,326	3,098,500	1,082,100	2,016,400	197,687	210,066	1,813,713	1,806,333
1971	7,010,216	4,466,219	2,168,740	2,297,479	225,244	239,349	2,072,235	2,058,130
1981	8,690,600	5,735,796	2,882,561	2,853,235	279,731	292,317	2,573,504	2,560,918
1991	9,014,879	6,002,474	2,804,872	3,197,602	313,496	327,598	2,884,106	2,870,004
2001	9,804,507	6,470,974	3,041,358	3,429,616	336,239	351,367	3,093,377	3,078,249
2015	14,056,021	9,276,960	4,686,466	4,590,494	449,409	NA	4,141,085	NA

Sources:
* For figures of 1961, 1971 & 1991 in columns 1, 2, 3, 4 Census of respective years have been used and figures for 1981, 2001 and 2015 have been projected by appropriate method of projection.
* Figures for 1991, Census of India, 1991 (Assam part), series-4, Part-IV, A-C series, Pp. 278, 350 and 426.
* Figures of 1961, 1971, 1981, 2001 and 2015 for the columns-5 have been estimated on the basis of proportion of Children Not-attending school to Child labour found in 1991 Census report.
* Figures in column-7 have been derived by subtracting the figures in column-5 from column-4.
* Figures in Col. 6 and Col. 8; Annual Report of the Ministry of Labour, 1996-97 (Delhi) Govt. of India Publication, P.100. And the figures for 2001 for columns 6 and 8 have been estimated using the proportions of the year of 1991.

child-workers (col.5). The 2001 and 2015 figures for columns 1, 2, 3 and 4 have been estimated by using appropriate methods of population projection; and figures for the columns 5 and 7 (for 2001 and 2015 population) have been estimated on the basis of proportion of children-not-attending school, nowhere children and child labourers found in 1991 census reports for the state.

Table - 3.1 shows that the magnitude of child labourers has increased from 1.97 lakh in 1961 to 2.25 lakh in 1971 to 2.79 lakh in 1981 and then to 3.13 lakh in 1991, which is nearly 10 per cent of the total children not-attending the school in the respective years. By the turn of 2001 A.D. the size of child labour force in Assam is expected to cross 3.36 lakh and by 2015 A.D the magnitude may inflate to 4.49 lakh.

Such an increasing trend of child labour force over the years has been found associated with human population explosion in the rural areas of the state. So, it has been creating infinite human problems and undesirable effects on the socio-economic milieu and natural environment.

Unless proper socio-economic measures are taken, in addition to the existing legal and administrative steps, the child labour problem of the state will further worsen and shall defy its solution.

Child labour in the State by Level of Work Participation and Gender

A classification of child labourers in the state has been made according to their level of work-participation, such as, main and marginal workers and by genders. Such categorisation reveals that the magnitude of main-workers in the state has increased from 1.59 lakh to 2.71 lakh during 1961-2001; while the volume of marginal workers has increased from 38 thousand to 65 thousand during the same period (Table-3.2, cols 2 and 3).

An important observation made in the study is that majority (80%) of the child labourers in the state have been working as main workers and the trend is continuing to be unabated.

Both in education and work-participation gender bias has been observed. It is found to be in favour of male child. Census of 1991

Table–3.2
Total Child-Labour force, Main, Marginal, Male & Female Child Labourers in Assam, 1961-2015.

Year	Total Child Labourers	Main Child Workers	Marginal Child Workers	Male Child Workers (Main + Marginal)	Female Child Workers (Main + Marginal)
	Col-I	Col-2	Col-3	Col-4	Col-5
1961	197,687	159,434	38,253	125,532	72,155
1971	225,244	181,659	43,585	143,030	82,214
1981	279,731	225,603	54,128	177,630	102,101
1991	313,496	252,863	60,633	198,988	114,508
2001	336,239	271,176	65,063	213,512	122,727
2015	449,000	341,240	107,760	285,115	163,885

Sources: * Figures in Col-I have been taken from Table-3.1

* Figures of 1961, 1971, 1981, 2001 and 2015 in columns 2, 3, 4, 5 have been estimated on the basis of proportion of Main Child-Workers to Marginal Child workers and Male to Female Child-Workers found in 1991 Census book.

* For Figures of 1991, Census of India (Assam Part) series-4, Part-IV, A-C Series, pp. 278, 350 and 426.

also unveils such a fact. According to its report 64 per cent child labourers are male and only 36 per cent are females. It is really very unfortunate that the work force participation rate of female-children has increased over the years (Table-3.2).

Structural Pattern of Child labourers

Out of 2290 households surveyed in 35 villages spread over five zones within the Sivasagar district of Assam only 187 households are found to have sent their children (5-14) to work for others as child labour. The village zones have been named according to their nearest town /urban centres. These are given below:

Name of the Zone	No of villages	No of h/hs	No of h/hs supplying child labour	No of child labourers
i Amgurie	5	121	28	41
ii Nazira	6	894	36	36
iii Sivasagar-Gaorisagar	6	269	28	37
iv Sonari	6	456	24	28
v Nitai-Demow	12	550	71	103
Total	35	2290	187	245

Table shows that certain households (h/hs) have supplied more than one child labourer for working outside. An analysis of the socio-economic background of the child labourers and their families has been given below:

Parents' literacy has been found to have greater impact on the literacy level as well as on work- participation of their children. It has been observed that the higher the level of parents' literacy, the lower is the possibility of work participation of their children. Education helps in acquiring knowledge, improving the work-skill, efficiency and the capability of children. So, literate parents have been found to favour sending their children to school for such positive gains of education. The positive attitude of parents toward education and educating their children, inter alia, have almost neutralised the forces of economic compulsion which cause to put a child into work.

During field trips it has been observed that among the child labour supplier families, the largest majority of the parents (86%) are illiterate, and even the remainder 13 per cent too are below matric standard. Among the female heads, out of 35, 80 per cent (28) are illiterates. A matriculate male head is found to be nil, while a matriculate female-family head too is a rare phenomenon in such families to which child labourers belong to (Table-3.3).

In cases of 152 male-headed families, in total 133 (87.5%) male-heads have been found to be illiterate (Table-3.3). None of the heads of these households has been observed to be optimistic, and opting to go-in-for adult education. Mainly, abject family poverty, inter alia, has discouraged them in all fronts. In spite of changing socio-cultural and technological environment in the urban periphery, the literacy level of these parents is very poor either because of civilization gap or inter-generational cycle of exploitation and deprivation or otherwise.[1]

(a) Literacy Level of the Child labourers

The poor level of parents' literacy has been found to have adverse impact on the child labourers. Most of the child labourers (90%) have not completed middle school level education. For, they have been sent to work by their illiterate parents at early ages. Thus, education of the children is adversely affected.

Table-3.4 unveils that work participation of illiterate children is as high as 37.55 per cent and it is much lower (9.39%) with children having even below matric level education.

Again, compared to male children, work participation of the female children is high at the below primary level education (40.96%). But, it is much lower at below matric level education (4.82%). Thus, gender bias in education is evident with a clear disfavour to female children. Such biasness, perhaps, is the out come of priority given on education of male children over the female children.

Table–3.3
Literacy Level of Male and Female Heads of the Child Labour Owning Families in Sivasagar District.

Literacy Level	No. of Male Heads	Cumulative % of literate Male Heads	No. of Female Heads	Cumulative % of Literate Female Heads	Cumulative % of illitrate Male Heads	Cumulative % of illitrate Female Heads
Col-1	Col-2	Col-3	Col-4	Col-5	Col-6	Col-7
i. Up to Primary level	4	12.50	2	20.00	87.50	80.00
ii. Middle level	7	9.87	2	14.28	90.13	85.72
iii. Below Matric	8	5.26	2	8.57	94.74	91.43
iv. Matriculate	-	0.00	1	2.86	94.74	97.14
v. Graduate	-	0.00	-	0.00	100.00	100.00
vi. Total literates	19		7			
vii. Total No. of Heads.	152		35			
viii. % of Literates	12.50		20.00			
ix. % of illiterates	87.50		80.00			
x. % Total	100.00		100.00			

Source: Primary Field Survey data in Sivasagar district.

(b) Age Composition:

Analysis of age composition of the child labourers reveals, with the increase in biological age of children, their work participation rate increases. Table - 3.5 shows, largest number of child labourers (67%) falls in the age group of 13-15 years.

But, in the 13-15 age group the percentage share of work-participation of male child labourers is larger (69%) than the female child workers (62%). Fall in percentage share of female child at higher ages is due to physiological disadvantage and early marriages.

Analysis of age and sex-wise distribution of child labourers in Table- 3.5 reveals that in 5-7 years age group the incidence of child labour is the lowest (0.41%). But, in 13-15 years age group it is as high as 67 per cent. The mean age ($\overline{x}$) of child labourers has been estimated to be 12.84 years.[2]

It has also been found that disadvantaged children start working from eight or nine years of their age. However, as unveiled in Table-3.6, most of them (72%) enter into the world of work before the age of 12 years. Majority of the unpaid female child labourers (56%) have been found start working from eight /nine years of their age.

The proportion of child labourers starting work before they are eight years has been found to be insignificant (5.31%). But, in case of self-employed child labourers it figures at 6.67 per cent. It has been observed that starting of work at early ages is basically a rural phenomenon. Attempt has been made to flash-out the reasons behind it in Chapter 5

(c) Location of Work: Rural-Urban Engagement of Child labourers:

Distribution of working children by their place of work and employment pattern presented in tabular form in Table - 3.7 unveils that most of the child labourers (73%) get themselves employed in rural areas to which they originate. Only 27 per cent find themselves in urban centres as they haunt for better earnings.

Table–3.4
Literacy Lavel of the Child Labourers

Literacy level/ Cadestral village area	Amgurie		Nazira		Sonari		Near to Sivasagar town		Nitai Demow		Male Total %		Femlae Total %		Grand Total	
	M	F	M	F	M	F	M	F	M	F	M	%	F	%	(+ F)	%
i. Below Primary level	5	2	3	6	18	6	14	3	18	17	58	(35.81)	34	(40.96)	92	(37.55)
ii. Primary level	10	7	6	3	2	-	8	1	13	18	39	(24.07)	29	(34.94)	68	(27.75)
iii. Middle level	12	2	15	3	2	-	8	-	9	11	46	(28.39)	16	(19.28)	62	(25.31)
iv. Below Matric	3	-	-	-	-	-	2	1	14	3	19	(11.73)	4	(4.82)	23	(9.39)
Total	30	11	24	12	22	6	32	5	54	49	162	(100.00)	83	(100.00)	245	(100.00)
% to Total Child Labourers												(66.12)		(33.88)		100.00

Source: Primary Field Survey data

M	=	162
F	=	83
Total	=	245

Table–3.5

Age & Sex-wise Distribution of Child Labourers of the Surveyed Villages in Sivasagar District.

		Total Male Child Labourers	% to total Male Child Labourers	Total Female Child Labourers	% total Female Child Labourers	Total (M+F) Child Labourers	% to total	Cumulative percentage
		1	2	3	4	5		6
Age Break up	5-7	1	0.62	-	-	1	0.41	0.41
	8-10	14	8.64	16	19.28	30	12.24	12.65
	11-12	35	21.6	15	18.07	50	20.41	33.06
	13-15	112	69.14	52	62.65	164	66.94	100
	Total % to total	162 (66.12)	100	83 (33.88)	100	245 (100.00)	100	

Source:- As in Table - 3.4

* **Note:-** Mean Age ($\overline{X}$) = 12.84

M	=	162
F	=	83
Total	=	245

Table–3.6

Distribution of Child Labourers of the Surveyed Villages by Age of Starting work & Nature of work.

Work Starting Age-Group	Self-enployed Child-Labourers				Wage-Paid Child-Labourers				Unpaid Child Labourers				Total Child-Labourers		
	M	% to total	F	% to total	M	% to total	F	% to total	M	% to total	F	% to total	M+F	% to total	cf %
below-5	-	-	-		-	-	-	-	-	-	-	-	-	-	
5-7	2	6.67	-		4	3.36	7	10.45	-	-	-	-	13	5.31	(5.31)
8-9	12	40	-		15	12.61	18	26.86	5	38.46	9	56.25	59	24.08	(29.39)
10-11	10	33.33	-		60	50.42	27	40.3	3	23.08	5	31.25	105	42.86	(72.25)
12-13	6	20	-		40	33.61	15	22.39	5	38.46	2	12.5	68	27.75	(100.00)
Total	30	(100.00)	-		119	100.00	67	100	13	100.00	16		245	100.00	
% of total	12.24				48.57		27.35		5.31		6.53	→	100.00		

Source :-Primary field survey Data

The other reasons of such migration of rural originated child labourers to urban centres, perhaps, are lack of employment opportunity in native villages, expanding and better job facilities in the urban areas.

Table - 3.7 shows that out of 180 child labourers in rural areas, as many as 151 or 84 per cent are wage-paid, while 11 or 6 per cent are unpaid, and the rest 18 or 10 per cent are self-employed. Similarly out of 65 child labourers in urban areas, 35 or 53 per cent are wage-paid, 18 or 27 per cent are unpaid and 12 or 18 per cent are self-employed.

Thus, both in rural and urban areas, the wage-paid child labourers form the largest group. For, perhaps, child labourers as well as their parents give top priority on immediate economic benefit from the services rendered.

(d) Nature of Works:

Child labourers of each surveyed areas (5 areas) have been categorised into three groups according to their nature of work, such as-

(i) self-employed

(ii) wage-paid and

(iii) unpaid child labourers.

Again, on the basis of their work link with skill generation process, the child labourer found have been classified into-

(i) unskilled

(ii) semi-skilled and

(iii) skilled labourers.

Table- 3.8 shows classification of the nature of work performed by the sample child labourers.

Child labourers reported as skilful in performing household work and agricultural activities have been classed as semi-skilled and those who have tendency to acquire skill in the process of working or in apprentice work but have not completed the apprenticeship period have been classed as skilled-child labourers.

Table–3.7

Distribution of Child Labourers by Location of work & Employment Pattern of the Surveyed villages in Sivasagar District

Child Labourers Employment pattern	Rural Area					
	RM	% to Rural Child Labourers	RF	% to Rural Child Labourers	R (M+F)	% to total
(1)	(2)	(3)	(4)	(5)	(6)	(7)
Self employed	18	(10.00)	-	-	18	(10.00)
wage paid	93	(51.67)	58	(32.22)	151	(83.89)
Unpaid	3	(1.67)	8	(4.44)	11	(6.11)
Total	114	(63.34)	66	(37.66)	180	(100.00)
% to total (245)	(46.53)		(26.94)		=73.47	

(Contd...)

Table Contd...

Child Labourers Employment pattern	Urban Area						Rural-Urban Total	
	UM	% to Urban Child Labourers	UF	% to Urban Child Labourers	U (M+F)	% to total	Total (M+F) Child Labourers	% to total
(1)	(8)	(9)	(10)	(11)	(12)	(13)	(14)	(15)
Self employment	12	(18.46)	-	-	12	(18.46)	30	(15.00)
Wage paid	26	(40.00)	9	(13.85)	35	(53.85)	186	(12.24)
Unpaid	10	(15.38)	8	(12.31)	18	(27.69)	29	(75.92)
Total	48	(73.84)	17	(26.26)	65	(100.00)	245	(11.84)
% to total (245)	(19.59)		(6.94)		=(26.53)	73. 47 + 26.53 = 100.00		(100.00)

Source:- As given in total - 3.6

M	=	162
F	=	83
Total	=	245

Table–3.8

Distribution of Child Labourers by Type of Activity & Nature of Work

Nature of Work	Self-Employed				Wage Paid				Unpaid					
	M	% to total Male	F	% to total Female	M	% to total Male	F	% to total Female	M	% to total Male	F	% to total Female	M + F Total	% to total
	(1)	(2)	(3)	(4)	(5)	(6)	(7)	(8)	(9)	(10)	(11)	(12)	(13)	(14)
1. Unskilled	22	(73.33)	-	-	70	(58.82)	44	(65.67)	12	(92.31)	15	(93.75)	163	(66.53)
2. Semi Skilled	-	-	-	-	38	(31.93)	20	-29.85)	1	(7.69)	1	(6.25)	60	(24.41)
3. Skilled	8	(2.67)	-	-	11	(9.25)	3	(4.48)	-	-	-	-	22	(8.98)
Total =	30	-100			119	(100.00)	67	(100.00)	13	(100.00)	16	(100.00)	245	(100.00)
% to total	12.24 + NIL = 12.24				48.57 + 27.35 = 75.92				5.31 + 6.53 = 11.84					100.00

Source:- Primary Field Survey Data.

Accordingly, unskilled child labours, as Table - 3.8 reveals, have been found to be the largest majority (66.53%) in all types of activity, followed by semi-skilled and unpaid child labourers.

(e) Sectoral Structure of Employment of the Child labourers:

Categorisation of child labourers under certain heads /sectors has been found to associate with difficulties. For, child labourers are involved in various activities. The complexity of the problem is that in a calendar year a child labourer involves in more than one activity and/or change her/his occupation or cease to work. So, only regular working child labourers in different activities other than at her/his own home found in the surveyed villages have been taken into account and considered for the analysis.

Thus, the economic activities to which the child labourers are found associated have been classified into five main sectors of employment, such as:

(i) agricultural sector,

(ii) construction sector,

(iii) trade and commerce,

(iv) domestic work (wage paid) and

(v) household servants (paid and unpaid).

A child employed under a master other than her/his parents as agricultural worker (who has also to perform household works), and/or as tea-garden worker has been included under the agricultural sector.

A wage-paid child working in brick-kiln and /or as jugali to masons has been categorised as child-labourer under construction sector.

Children employing themselves, in carpentry, manufacturing, car-workshops, fish, cloths, vegetable business and car driving, in fishing and butchery have been included under the sector of trade and commerce. Children working as hotel boy or employed in grocery shops have also been covered under this sector.

Under the domestic-work sector a child working on daily-wage basis, and that who performs only domestic works other than agricultural deeds, but purely as casual labour has been listed.

A retainer, bonded labourer and /or a permanent labour of 5-15 age group who has to perform all sorts of household-drudgery has been classified as household-servant.

Accordingly, tabular presentation of the sectoral classification of child labourers employed (in Table 3.9) unveils that more than half of the child labour force is being absorbed in agricultural sector (31.83%) and in domestic works (26.94%). Of the rest about 18 per cent is getting employed in trade and commerce, 15 per cent in brick-kilns and building construction etc., while 8 per cent is sucked-up for household slavery.

It has also been observed that with the advancement of biological age, the volume of child labour force participating in economic activities is growing. This is, perhaps, because of the growing ability and physical fitness of the child labourers to perform the allotted and /or available works, a bit properly. The Table -3.9 reveals again that in lower age-group, viz 5-7 years, child labourers participating in work constitutes only 0.41 per cent of the total child labour-force engaged in various economic activities; while in 13-15 age group they form about 67 per cent of the universe.

(f) Gender bias

A simple measure of proportion, such as, female child-labourers to male-child labourers presented in Tables- 3.10 and 3.11 are well reflecting the gender inequalities in respect of (i) education, (ii) economic opportunity opened to female child-labourers and (iii) the achievements of and inequalities in human development in the state (or society).

The Tables (Table 3.10 and 3.11) have shown that male child labourers are preferred most for employment in various economic activities except that for performing household chores. Lower status accorded to girls may be one of the reasons behind it.

Table–3.9
Sectoral Employment Structure of Child Labourers in the Sruveyed Villages in Sivasagar District

	Sectors of Employment										Total			
Age break -up	Agricultural		Construction		Trade & Commerce		Domestic Work		Household Servant					
	M	F	M	F	M	F	M	F	M	F	M	F	Total (M+F)	% to total
	(1)	(2)	(3)	(4)	(5)	(6)	(7)	(8)	(9)	(10)	(11)	(12)	(13)	(14)
5-7	1	-	-	-	-	-	-	-	-	-	1	-	1	(0.41)
8-10	1	-	-	2	5	-	6	11	2	3	14	16	30	(12.24)
11-12	7	7	4	2	13	-	9	6	2	0	35	15	50	(20.41)
13-15	37	25	24	5	26	-	22	12	3	10	112	52	164	(66.94)
Total =	46	32	28	9	44	0	37	29	7	13	162	83	245	(100.00)
% to total	18.77	13.06	11.43	3.67	17.96	0	15.1	11.84	2.86	5.31	(66.12)	(33.88)	⟶	100
%(M+F)=	(31.83)		(15.10)		(17.96)		(26.94)		(8.17)		(100.00)			

Source: Primary Feild Survey Data.

Several other factors, such as religion, culture, and the geographical nature of the locality affect the lives of female child labourers. For such reasons, female child labourers have been observed to suffer more in terms of educational, health, economic and legal opportunities in comparision to their male counterparts. Whatever be the reasons behind, out of 245 total universe of child labourers in the current study, 83 or 34 per cent are female and 162 or 66 per cent male child labourers.

In rural areas, - in the place of origins of the child labourers, employments of both male (46.53%) and female (26.94%) child labourers have been found to be large in comparision to their engagement in urban centres (Table-3.10). It indicates a fact that of the total child labour force generated in the rural areas of the state, some 19.59 per cent male and 6.94 per cent female child labourers migrate to urban centres for earning their family bread. It is expected that mobility of the child labourers would be inching up with the growth of rural population in the state.

Table- 3.11 unveils that female child labourers are preferred most for household-works followed by the agricultural sector.

The households (h/hs) of the villages peripheral to an industrial or a commercial centre, such as, Nazira and Amguri have supplied higher number of female child labourers than the villages of other industrial or commercial centres.

Non- employment of child labour has been observed in the sample villages around Sivasagar -Gaurisagar and Sonari town in construction activity. Similarly, employment of child labourers has been found completely absent in certain other activities in certain other areas as well. For example, in trade & commerce in the villages around the Sivasagar town and Gaurisagar semi-urban area, in construction work, trade & commerce in the rural sites both in Nazira and Amgurie engagement of female child labourers have not been found. Perhaps, the social traditions of these localities and racial customs and beliefs do not allow them to do so.

Table–3.10
Percentage Distribution of Child Labourers, Location - wise and Gender bias

Employment Pattern	Area & Gender - wise Distribution.											
	Male Child labourers					Female Child labourers						
	RM	% total	UM	% to total	% to total Male Child labourers	RF	% to total	UF	% to total	% to total Female Child labourers	M+F	% to total
	(1)	(2)	(3)	(4)	(5)	(6)	(7)	(8)	(9)	(10)	(11)	(12)
Self Employed	18	15.79	12	25	18.52	-	-	-	-	-	30	12.24
Wage paid	93	81.58	26	54.16	73.46	58	87.88	9	52.94	80.72	186	75.92
Unpaid	3	2.63	10	20.84	8.02	8	12.12	8	47.06	19.28	29	11.84
Total	114	100.00	48	100.00	10.00	66	-	17	100.00	100.00	245	100.00
% to Total	46.53		19.59		66.12	26.94	-	6.94		=33.88→100.00		

Source: Primary Field Survey Data.

	R	U	Total
Male	114	48	162
Female	66	17	83
Total	180	65	245

(g) Gender bias in Education

Though the gap in educational aspirations between different social groups is narrowing rapidly, in case of poorer families such aspirations give unequal attention to girls and boys. The gender bias in educating children has been found to be so strong during the field trip that necessity and usefulness of female education makes little sense to child labour owning families. To measure such gender bias in education an estimation has been made which is shown in Table 3.11.

As shown in the Table that 97.07 female child labourers in activity against 100 male primary educated child labour have acquired education up to primary level. But the figure suddenly dropped to 38.80 at middle level and 0.057 at below matric level. This can be regarded as most damaging discrimination for the girls in the matter of education.[3]

For, it denies the girls not only taking education but also forbids them to break the vicious circle of ignorance, exploitation, shackles of servitude and improve their lives through education. Thus, the North-Indian apathetic outlook towards female child-education is prevalent in socio-economically poor and backward pockets of the society.

Secondly, whereas elementary education is not a priority either for an alibi of resource crunch or agrarian type of society, so school drop outs of female children is very high at this stage.

Thirdly, even the social reformers did little to challenge the belief that knowledge was ultimately the preserve and responsibility of the privileged few during the last 50 years of independence. Besides, Left-movement too ignored education and believed that Maati (land) rather than Gyna (knowledge) was the crucial means of production, which the rural poor most needed.[4]

Further, it has been observed that enough schools, teachers and text books and the free education system are the necessary corollaries, but not entirely sufficient for ensuring required enrolment of children in the schools. For, the poorer the family is, the more difficult it is to bear the direct costs for books and clothing

Table–3.11

Gender bias in Education & Employment of Child Labour.

Cadestral Village Area Around	Number of Girls For 100 Boys in Activities								Total in Activity (5-141)
	Educational level				Sectors				
	illiterate	Primary	Middle	Below Matric	Agri	Construc-tion	Trade & Commerce	House hold Work	
1. Demow - Nitai	90.6	226.18	186.33	8.45	34.96	186.18	19.72	26.25	111.23
2. Sivasagar Town & Gaurisagar	25.68	27.82	12.36	0	12.36	NIL	0	50.54	21.52
3. Sonari	34.98	0	NIL	NIL	34.96	NIL	NIL	26.25	31.48
4. Nazira	204.47	51.17	20.45	NIL	NIL	0	0	409.17	51.08
5. Amguri	80.52	75.49	14.21	0	120.79	0	0	241.51	41.31
Total	62.08	97.07	38.8	0.057	67.42	37.65	2.49	109.57	56.14

Source: Computed from field survey Primary data.

* Computation Method - Girls in Activity per thousand in 0-14 age group divided by Boys in Activity per thousand in 0-14 age group x 100.

and the opportunity cost of sending them to school. In most cases the child-labour-owning parents are found to assess the opportunity cost of non-availability of their children for household chores as higher than the benefits to the family from their education.

Where resources are limited, priority is found given to education of the sons. In fact, with such a bias-ness, education remains to be a middle class property and as means of exploitation, rather than becoming a means for enhancement of material production.

All such facts unveil a great gender bias against the education of female children in poorer families of the state. So, a benign watchfulness needs to be preferred and action requires to be started to alleviate the poverty in order to meet the challenge of female education as well as exploitative child labour practices in the state.

Notes and References

1. IGIDR (2000) *India Development Report,* 2000; (Delhi) Kirit S. Parikh edited, IGIDR, p. 65.

2. Note:- A similar result has been found by K.R. Pillai in a study in Kerala state.

   See - Reddy, Y.S. (edited, 1999) *Child Labour,* (New Delhi), Anmol Publications, p. 156

3. The Mahbub Ul-Haq Human Development Centre (2000), *Human Development in South Asia, 2000*; (New York), Oxford University Press, p. 33

4. Centre for Development Economics (2000), *Public Report on Basic Education in India* (New Delhi), Oxford University Press, p. 134

4

Economics of Child Labour

Social scientists are not unanimous in their views on children entering in the world of economic activity as child labour. It is often argued that from social point of view child labour is a process of skill acquisition and craftsmanship development. So, in an agricultural family, child labour is an apprentice to such an enterprise. From the sociological view point child labour is a process of socialisation, a way of assimilation and adjustment with the prevailing socio-economic environment of the society.[1]

Some others consider full participation of a child into work as better than that of marginal child labour. Because, a child in the former type of work learns skill and becomes self reliant; but the later type of work does not mould the child into productive adult, nor it enhances the size of family income with adequate skill acquisition.

So, it is currently believed that child labour practices might be exploitative, but such practices positively contribute towards production, family income and social gains in general. Due to prevalence of such attitude and philosophy, inter alia, abolition of child labour practices in the country has become quite impossible.

But, on welfare ground, child labour is the worst kind of exploitation of children, waste of future human resources and deprivation of children from their due rights. For, human rights activists, child labour deforms the child psychology and it amounts to violation of human rights.[2] For, a society committed to improving the lives of its people, must also ensure equal rights to that section of children who have started their lives as child labourer. But, the complexity of the subject addresses many questions, such as, whether child labour is simply an issue of age, or hard labour, or income related problem or a socio-cultural problem or much more than that.

Any research on economics of child labour in the background of tradition- bound Under-developed economy would surely give paradoxical results. So, a few hypotheses relating to economics of child labour, in the context of the economy of Assam have been framed and these are tested by analysing the field data from the district of Sivasagar, Assam.

The Hypothesis

(i) It has been hypothesised that supply of and demand for child labour are mutually reinforcing.

(ii) That child labour is a necessary evil. The employer, the society and the individual family whom a child labourer belongs to, all are positively benefited.

(iii) That child labourers are satisfied with their task of doing work while earning livelihood for own-self and the family and their motives of entering the labour market are fulfilled.

(iv) The welfare measures of the government. for poor families have failed to reduce child labour in rural Assam.

Demand for and Supply of Child labour

In the absence of glaring industrial development due mainly to slower growth of manufacturing and processing units and industrial infrastructures, Assam is not experiencing large employment of children in hazardous works, found elsewhere in the country, such as, fire works making in Sivaski (Tamilnadu), Jem polishing in Joypur (Rajasthan), Glass making in Firozabad, Lock making in Aligarh, Brass-ware making in Maradabad, Pottery making in Khurja (all in U.P). But, the pitiable working conditions and the degree of exploitation of child labourers in the non-manufacturing informal and unorganised household sectors in the state are of such dimensions that they deserve equal gravity, importance and close observation of the social scientists as in other regions.

(a) Demand Side

The total number of child labourers (in 5-14 age group) employed in the state has increased from 1.97 lakh in 1961 to 3.13 lakh in 1991 and it is expected to cross 3.36 lakh in 2001 A.D. as shown in Table 3.1. It has been observed that the demand for child labourers in informal and household sectors of the state emanates from the necessity of performing agricultural and allied activities, household chores, menial works in hotels, shops, dhabas, commercial establishments, workshops & small plantations, to render little bit of services in cars, buses and three-wheelers.

Child labourers employed in households and/or agricultural activities do not normally deal with dangerous machines. But, such children as domestic servants are often ill treated, beaten, overloaded with works, asked to perform low and ignoble works and to work for longer hours. Similarly, in most cases, children employed in hotels, shops, dhabas, commercial establishments, cars, buses and/or workshops have been the victims of (sex) abuse, malnutrition and maltreatment. Despite several labour laws and other efforts of protection, many of such child labourers have been found surviving at the mercy of their masters.

Though the state is confronting a high level of youth unemployment (16.65 lakh in 2000 as shown in Table - 4.1) yet the increasing demand for labourers in the informal and unorganised sectors of the state has been found being filled up by both local and immigrant child labourers. The plight of child labourers (including the migrant child labourers) has been found to be deplorable as most of them are forced to do the works of an adult worker at lower wages and remain separated from their parents.

Table–4.1
Unemployment Rate for Assam as % to Total Population & Total Labour Force, 1961-2001

Unemployment Rate as % to Total Population of the State				Unemployment Rate as % to Total Labour force in the state				
Year	Total Population (in lakhs)	No. of Job-seekers Recorded in Live-Register (in lakhs)	% of Unemployment to total Population	Year	Total Labour Force (in lakhs)	% of Labour Force to total Population	No. of Job seekers on Live-Register (in lakh)	% of Unemploy-ment to total Labour Force
(1)	(2)	(3)	(4)	(5)	(6)	(7)	(3)	(4)
1961	108	0.316	0.29	1961	46.44	43	0.316	0.7
1971	146	0.948	0.64	1971	41.00	30	0.948	2.3
1981	180	3.730	2.07	1981	64.96	36.07	3.73	5.7
1991	224	10.52	4.69	1991	80.80	36.09	10.52	13.01
1995	244	11.47	4.70				11.47	
1996	249	12.84	5.16				12.84	
1997	255	10.02	3.93	1997	92.03	36.09	10.02	10.88
2000	262	16.35	5.89	2000	98.16	36.09	16.35	16.65
2001	266	17.50	6.58	2001			17.50	

Source: i. Report of the Labour Minister, Assam, on 6th Sept/1983
ii. Report of the Labour Minister, Assam, on 5 March/ 1990
iii. Economic Survey 1 Assam, 1997-98.
iv. Report of the Labour Minister, Assam in the Assam Tribune, 27 June, 2001.

Employers prefer child labourers for several reasons.

(i) A Child labourer can be employed at lower wage rate.

(ii) They do not dare to raise any objection against exploitation, low wage, longer hours of work, bad food etc.

(iii) They can be asked to perform any low and ignoble services.

In a commercial establishment, such as, hotel, dhaba, nursing home etc, a child labour is demanded for performing the low and ignoble deeds and usually for day-long services. Such employers are reported to have good understanding with the local labour inspector(s). No commercial establishment is found to display in a Notice-Board, as per labour laws, the number of labourers employed, their age, nature of business undertaken and the name of the local labour inspector.[3] In the present study, the conditions of 21 (8.5%) child labourers employed in commercial establishments in the same areas have been investigated.

Demand for child labourers in rural sectors of the state arises for performing the agricultural and allied activities and for running the small plantations. The cases of 77 (31.4%) child labourers engaged in such activities have been investigated. In this study, the demand for child labour in agricultural sector is found to be perennial.

The largest quantum of demand for child labourer is found to have come from households to work as domestic servants. The sample of child labourers for this segment accounts for 35.9 per cent (88 Nos.) of the total sample child labourers taken in the present study. Of this 88, 12 (4.9%) child labourers work as unpaid servants (Table 4.2).

Extreme poverty and ignorance of the parents are found to be the compelling reason for sending children to work for others. Most of the children of such poverty-stricken families have been found to enter into labour force at their earliest childhood, at the age of six or seven years. Such a high urgency for employment on the part of the children themselves and their penetrability into labour market have made the constitutional mandate, international commitments, adoption of the convention of the rights of the children (CRC) in 1992, and the Government of India's deposition of Instruments of accession to the convention for the abolition of child labour practices almost null and void.

Table–4.2
Sector/Activity-wise Classification of the Sample Child labourers in Sivasagar District

Sector/ Activity	No. of Self-employed lab.	No. of Wage paid Child lab.	No. of Unpaid Child lab.	No. of Total Child lab.	% to Total
Col-1	Col-2	Col-3	Col-4	Col-5	Col-6
Agriculture & Allied					
1 Fishing	10	-		10	4.08
2 Agriculture	6	-		6	2.45A
3 Agri & Domestic works	-	41	8	49	20.00A
4 Piggery	1			1	0.41
5 Tea-garden Lab.	-	22		22	8.98A
Trade and Commerce					
6 Cloth business	1			1	0.41
7 Grocery business	2			2	0.82C
8 Butchery	1			1	0.41
9 Veg. business	4			4	1.63
10 Furniture works	2			2	0.82C
11 Asists in Begging		1	-	1	0.41
12 Hotel boy		8	6	14	5.71C
13 Handiman		2		2	0.82
14 Car driving		1		1	0.41
15 Fish business	3			3	1.22
Manufacturing and Construction					
16 Workshop & Manufacturing			3	3	1.22C
17 Jugali/Building construction.		21		21	8.57
18 Brick Kilns		14		14	5.71
Household works					
19 Domestic works (on wages)		72		72	29.39
20 House servant		4	12	16	6.53
	30 (12.24%)	186 (75.92%)	29 (11.84%)	245	(100.00%)

* A = for Agriculturel activities.
* C = for commercial establishments.

As early entrants into the labour market, most of the child labourers have to bear the brunt of heavy workload. It causes stunted physical growth and shortening of working lives. Many of such child labourers that have now grown adult are found unable to work at 35-45, due to weak health and/or illness.

concomitantly, due to easy advantage of employing a child at relatively lower wage-rate, slackness of the labour inspecting department, lacuna and lethargy in implementing the Child Labour Act, 1986 and other legal measures, the employers in informal sectors have been tapping the opportunity to their maximum gain. So, the demand for child labour in the state as 'Cheap labour' is gradually soaring high.

(b) Supply Side

Poverty and illiteracy, inter alia, have come to be identified as the main determinants of supply of child labour in the state as elsewhere in the country and in Asia continent.[4] Child labour is also considered as 'forced labour' caused by parental poverty, socio-economic-cultural background and the living pattern of the parents.[5] For, poor parents in their struggle for survival push their children into labour market as a first hand remedy. So, child labour employment is seen more as an economic problem rather than anything else.

Secondly, bigger family size is found to be a contributing factor towards child labour. This phenomenon of bigger family size being very common in rural India the supply of child labour is of high magnitude from the rural areas.

Thirdly, population explosion caused by absence of desired demographic transition and very low-income level are keeping a section of the rural society to run along the vicious spiral of poverty, illiteracy and ignorance. These three variables are observed functioning as continuum resulting in increasing supply of child labour in the state.[6]

Historically, a high level of association between child labour supply in one hand and family poverty and illiteracy on the other has been observed in this state. In spite of serious efforts of poverty alleviation, the proportion of people living below poverty line has been increasing from 39.9 per cent in late 1950's to 49.3 per cent in early 1990's due to excessive growth of population in the state from 0.80 crores in 1951 to 2.24 crores in 1991 and 2.66 crores in 2001.[7]

Moreover, the number of children Not-attending the School, - the primary stock of child labour force has been increasing in the state from 20.16 lakh in 1961 to 31.97 lakh in 1991 and to 34.29 lakh as estimated for 2001 A.D. (Table - 3.1, Chapter III). The magnitude of redundant children, i.e. Non-student & Non-workers too has been increasing in the state due to lower demand for child labourers than its supply coming from the destitute families. So, International Labour Organisation (ILO) rightly opines that poverty is the greatest force creating and maintaining a steady flow of child labourers.[8]

Fourthly, not even one of 187 sample households (h/hs) supplying child labourers has received so far any kind of benefits from the Government welfare schemes under Swarnajayanti Gram Swarozgar Yojana (SGSY). Absence of family allowance to enable the poor parents to secure for their children adequate food and living/rest-place has also been observed. Under such circumstances poor families put their children to work for the survival and sustaining of the family and/or to maximize the family income. In fact, lack of supportive measures for the poorest families constituting the perennial source of child labour supply has been observed to be responsible, inter alia, for increasing trend of child labour supply in the state. In order to curb this increasing trend a social security pension scheme for the poorest families supplying child labourers in the state may be thought of. Such benefits should also be tagged with a clear responsibility of limiting the family size to such beneficiary families.

In most cases supply of child labour is observed to be positively related to the level of wages paid to a child labourer. For, increasing wage levels entice the non-student & non-workers in 5-14 age group to join the labour force; while a decrease in their wage rate too accentuates disaster to their lives. From close scrutiny of field survey data it has been observed that child labour supply is non-negative below the per capita per month (Pcpm) income range of Rs. 25 - 379 and non-positive in the Pcpm income range of Rs. 380 - 629 and nil beyond the Pcpm income of Rs. 629. As shown in Table - 4.3, each sample h/h of the mean ranges of Rs. 25 - 229, Rs. 230 - 379, Rs. 380 - 539, Rs. 540 - 629 and Rs.630- onward, has supplied on an average, 1.327, 1.341, 1.256, 1.00 and nil number of child labour, respectively. Hence, Rs. 380 - 539 becomes the break even income range (BEIR, Diagram No.-1) for the child labour supplying households indicating the fact that by increasing the Pcpm income to this level or decreasing the economic poverty, the magnitude of child labour supply could be contained to a large extent.

The phenomenon of positive supply of child labour (albeit with a decreasing trend) at the Rs. 540 - 629 income range implies, in addition to economic poverty some other social forces have been working behind the child labour supply. This is the reason why a family even from an income range below the break even range of income may not supply child labour.

For example, despite sizeable Pcpm income (in Rs. 540 - 629 income range) 5 (five) h/hs were found to have sent their minor children to work for wages. The reason of such behaviour are rooted in negative attitude to education, social backwardness and high attribution to income.

Fertility and family size have also been observed to be inversely related to family income level. Demographic trends of several countries and the development experience of developed countries show that higher income level of a family is resulting in not only lower fertility but less number of siblings also. [9] Such evidences support the logic that in the economically poor and socially uncultured region/ society, the top priority should be given on:

(i) the reduction of poverty, (ii) increase in family income, (iii) promotion of literacy rate and (iv) extension of health services, inter alia, in order to eliminate the exploitative child labour practices and the cyclical generation of child labour force.

Table–4.3
Statement Showing Average Supply of Child labour at Different Per Capita Per Month (Pcpm) Income Range of the Sample Households

Pcm Income Break up	No. of Sample h/hs in the cadestral village area of					Total No. of h/hs	Total No. of Child labour supplied	Average supply of Child Labour
	Amgurie	Nazira	Sonari	Sivsagar Town & Gorisagar	Nitai-Demow			
(1)	(2)	(3)	(4)	(5)	(6)	(7)	(8)	(9)
Rs. 25 - 229	9	10	16	11	15	61	81	1.327
Rs. 230 - 379	11	21	7	11	32	82	110	1.341
Rs. 380 - 539	8	5	1	4	21	39	49	1.256
Rs. 540 - 629	Nil	Nil	Nil	2	3	5	5	1.000
Rs. 630 - onward	Nil	Nil	Nil	Nil	Nil	Nil	Nil	Nil
Total	28	36	24	28	71	187	245	1.310

Source: Primary Field Survey Data.

Diagram no. 1

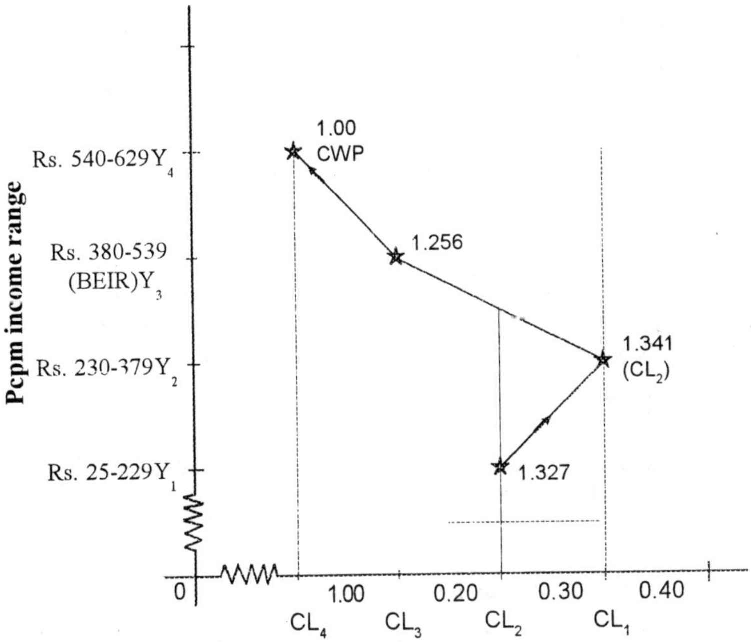

Average child labour supply by each sample h/hs

***Where CWP = Child labour supply curve**

CL_2 = Maximum child labour supply by 82 h/hs within the Pcpm income range of Rs. 230 - 379 is 110 Nos.

Child Labour: A Civil or Evil Practice

The issue of child labour as stated earlier in this chapter, has long been viewed with suspicion and indifference in all developing countries, including India until a dramatic change of views taking place in the last decade of the 20th century at the leadership of international organisations. For, while some viewed healthy work in childhood as social good, biological need and national gain, many others, considered it as social evil and national waste. Earning by a child labourer supports the family, maximize the family income of the poor and thus the individual family temporarily gains by it. The child also becomes self- dependent at her/his early life. Hence, many look at child labour practice as necessary evil; ------ an evil necessary for deterring the idle children from involving in anti social activity by keeping them engaged in productive works. Now, views have changed for the following reasons -

(a) Whatever benefit a society may derive, the practice of child labour has been condemned by all in international fora. For, it involves violation of human rights and negates the dignity of a child as human being.

Many countries of the world - poor and rich have been showing a new zeal and dynamism in taking initiatives for human rights and human development. India is not lagging behind as her Human Development Rank (HDI) is 128 in 2000 A.D.[10]

So, government of India passed a legislation to be effective from 28th September, 1993, with the objective of the constitution of National Human Rights Commission (NHRC), State Human Rights Commissions and Human Rights Courts (HRCs) for better protection of human rights and matters connected with it or incidental there to. While the NHRC was constituted in October, 1993, the Assam Human Rights Commission (AHRC) came into existence with five members and a secretary to it in 1996. The NHRC and AHRC are vocal against child exploitation and child labour practices.

The history of the movement for protection of human rights originates to adoption of 'Universal Declaration of Human Rights' by the United Nations in 1948. In its Charter, the United Nations (UNO) committed to ensure that no individual-regardless of gender, ethnicity or race - shall have her/his human rights abused or ignored. Every child, thus, as human being or as member of the human community has the rights to life, liberty, schooling, health care and equal dignity.[11] In the charter of the Universal Declaration of Human Rights (UDHR) in Article - 4 it has been proclaimed that -

> "No one shall be held in slavery or servitude; Slavery and the slave trade shall be prohibited in all forms."

Thus, the practice of child labour has been internationally outlawed as inhuman practice since long back. India has committed to honour these.

(b) Besides, as a signatory to the convention of the rights of the children, 1989 (CRC), the government of India has recognised the harsh reality of child labour and promised since 1996 to eliminate the child labour practices in the country. Under the convention of 1989, a child means every human being below the age of 18 years and whose best interest must be taken into account in all situations.[12] Thus, both the central and state governments are bound to set free all the child labourers in the country and end up the situations which cause/force children to put into the labour force.

(c) Apart from these, child labour is considered more as a social and economic evil, than a necessity on the following counts.

   (i) Mainly to avoid the harshness of grinding poverty young children are put into work. But, such economic necessity deprives the child of an opportunity for primary education, healthy growth and enjoyment of childhood. Child labour stunts the physical growth of the child, thwarts the child to suffer the health-hazards and injury and to bear the responsibility of family maintenance. All such factors interfere her/his normal development of morality and personality.

(ii) Child labour damages the health and vitality of the child. It shortens the longevity of the child and cause her/him to suffer from malnutrition and debility. Child labour brings about moral degradation and make the child vulnerable to various diseases.

(iii) Child labour leads to inefficient utilisation of labour power and results in low productivity. The worst effect of it is that it degenerates the human capital.

(iv) Child labour degrades the social order and norms, causes social turmoil, helps early procreation, spread veneral diseases, results in bigger family size and speedy population growth and population explosion.

Whether boon or bane to the society, exploitative child labour practice in the state has come to stay merely because of extreme family poverty and illiteracy of such people. Though paradoxical, so long these two problems-viz: family poverty and illiteracy continue to exist, elimination of child labour practices would be quite impossible. The increasing trend of excessive child labour supply over its demand confirms such hypothesis. A further deterioration of living standard of the poors would increase the number of redundant children to enter the labour market displacing a large volume of adult workers which may worsen the unemployment situation and the balance of the state economy.

Work Satisfaction, fulfilment of Aspirations and Motives of Child Labourers

(a) Dreams of school going and/or living a better life have often been found reflected in the faces and words of the child labourers. In fact, none of the child labourers has been satisfied with their life-style of doing work under the existing socio-economic compulsion of their families. But as many as 134 (54.6%) child labourers have expressed the views that in the absence of any better alternative they have to be satisfied with the present job and learn to live with it.

(b) In spite of the preparedness to sacrifice the parental care and love, to work hard and render day-long services under tough conditions, all the child labourers have stated that their motives and aspirations (and of their parents) have not been fulfilled. Most of the child labourers and their parents have reported that such children are working mainly under economic compulsion for supporting the family income or to provide a square meal to the family members, including the working children.

Whatever be the reasons of putting oneself as a child labour, the child and her/his parents are found to have certain motives behind it. Some of the aspirations underneath the going in for child-work have been found to be the following:

(i) to make oneself free from family debt,
(ii) recovery of mortgaged land,
(iii) purchasing of bullock, bicycle or thela etc.,
(iv) meeting of child's own expenses,
(v) getting educated under the care of the employer and/or
(vi) learning skill while the child is working.

It is to be noted that employment of their children in the economic activity has not improved financial condition or living standard of the parents except giving a very temporary relief. As such, the motives and aspirations, the long cherished goals of child labourers, behind their work participation, have been reported as gone unfulfilled forever.

For this reason again a large number of Child-domestic-workers have been found retiring from domestic servitude to work independently on daily wage basis. In either situations, childhood dreams have been found fading away. The possibility of generating more child labourers by such economically poor and socially backward families has been observed to be more imminent.

Classification of Child Labourers

On the basis of the type of economic activity taken up by the 245 child labourers surveyed (supplied by 187 Households), a

Table–4.4
Activity-wise Classification of Child labourers

No. of h/hs supplying child labourers	% to total h/hs	Classification of Child labourer based on Nature of work	No. of Child labourers supplied	% to total	Classification of Child labourers Activity wise			
					Agri & Allied	Trade & Coms.	Manufacturing & construction	h/h services
Col-1	Col-2	Col-3	Col-4	Col-5	Col-6	Col-7	Col-8	Col-9
141	75.40	Wege paid	186	75.92	63	12	35	76
22*	11.76	Un paid	29	11.84	8	6	3	12
24	12.84	Self- employed	30	12.24	17	13	-	-
187	100.00		245	100.00	88 (35.92)	31 (12.65)	38 (15.51)	88(35.92) (35.92)

* 4 (2.14%) h/hs have supplied 3 wage paid, one self-employed and 6 unpaid Child labourers.

Source: Primary field survey data from 5 zones in sivasagar district.

sector- wise classification, such as, child labourers in (i) Agri and Allied activities (88 or 35.9%), (ii) Trade and Commerce (31 or 12.6%) (iii) Manufacturing and Construction works (38 or 15.5%) and (iv) Household services (88 or 35.9%) has been made. This is shown in Table - 4.2.

Apart from this, on the basis of employment status, the sample child labourers have been classified as (i) Wage paid, (ii) Self-employed and (iii) Unpaid children. Accordingly, out of 245 child labourers 186 or 75.9 per cent (coming from 141 h/hs) have been found to be wage paid, 29 or 11.8 per cent (coming from 22 h/hs) as unpaid and 30 or 12.2 per cent (coming from 24 h/hs) as Self-employed (Table - 4.4).

Profile of Income, Expenditure and Saving of Wage paid and Self-employed Child Labourers:

The income expenditure and saving pattern of 186 Wage-paid and 30 Self-employed child laborers have been shown in Table 4.5.

Table–4.5
Average Monthly Income, Expenditure and Saving of the Wage paid and Self employed Child labours.

No. of Child Labours	Average Monthly Income per Child Labour (in Rs.)	Average Monthly personal expenditure (in Rs.)	Average Monthly saving per Child Labour (in Rs.)	Saving as % of Income
Col-1	Col-2	Col-3	Col-4	Col-5
i. Wagepaid=186	524.20	126.68	387.52	73.93
ii. Selfemployed=30	764.07	72.93	691.14	90.45
Total = 216	Av. 644.135	104.805	539.33	83.73

Source: Primary field survey data collected from sample child labour in Amgurie, Nazira, Sonari, Sivasagar and Nitai- Demow areas under Sivasagar district.

Income

Average monthly income has been estimated to be higher in case of self employed (Rs. 764) than the wage paid child labourers (Rs. 524).

Degree of variation of daily income of the working children has been observed to be high due to their variation of work-ability, age and opportunities.

The maximum average daily income for 115 or 61 per cent wage paid children out of 186, has been found below Rs. 20, for 46 or 25 per cent the wage rate is above Rs. 20, but below Rs. 30 a day. Only 25 or 14 per cent children have been able to earn in between Rs. 31 and Rs. 50 a day (Table - 6.7 Ch. VI). However, their daily earnings is much lower than the wages of adult workers.

Out of 30 self-employed children, 12 or 40 per cent have earned below Rs. 20 a day, while 15 or 50 per cent could earn within the range of Rs. 21 - Rs. 40, and 3 or 10 per cent earn above Rs. 40 per day, on an average (Table - 6.7. Ch. 6).

Profile of Expenditure

A wage paid child labourer spends a very small fraction (26.0%) of her/his income on her/his own. Almost the entire amount of income is spent on her/his family. Table-4.5 shows this phenomenon.

It has also been observed that out of 186 wage-paid child labourers, the personal expenditure of the (116 Nos.) child labourers who commute daily to and from work place, is higher than those (70 Nos) who stay at work place. It is because unlike the former type, most of the later type of child labourers do not get the opportunity of receiving their wage-money by themselves. Their parents directly take away the monthly salary/wage from their masters/employers on due date or even before.

However, the average monthly personal expenditures (Rs. 136.68 or 26.0 per cent of their monthly income) of the wage paid child labourers is found to be almost double the amount of such expenditures (Rs. 72.93 or 9.5 per cent of their monthly income) made by the self- employed children. It is because, many of the wage-paid child labourers have been found spending a part of their hard-earned meagre income on eatables, clothing, cinema-going, drinking and/or smoking. On the other hand, almost all the self-employed children (29 out of 30) are found to have taken the responsibility of maintaining their respective families. Of course, some of them are found to have developed the habit of consuming alcohol, smoking cigarette or biddies, gambling etc.

Savings

It is apparent from Table - 4.5 that wage paid and self-employed children have saved 73.9 per cent and 90.4 per cent of their average monthly income, respectively. This is saving only in accounting sense. In fact, the net-saving is nil. Because, whatever is saved has finally been spent on the family's sustenance. Thus, a plan to buy a pair of bullock, to release a plot of mortgaged land, if any; or to initiate a small business activity by a child labourer goes in vain. The fundamental fact is that unemployment situation of the adult workers and poor economic structure of such families continue to beget child labourers.

The question of income, expenditure and/or saving does not arise in case of 29 unpaid sample child labourers working as domestic servants. Though they do not earn anything for the family, the parents consider it as a relief. Because, in that case, the parents can shift the maintenance cost on the child to her/his employer.

Notes and References

1. Burra, Neera (1997), *Born to Work: Child Labour in India*; Delhi, Oxford University Press. P. Xi
2. Government of Assam, Deptt. of Personnel (B), Notification No. ABP/ 25/97/8 dt. 29th May, 1998, New Rule, 26-A.

(i) *Employment of Children*; Reproduced by AHRC (1999) in News Letter; Guwahati, AHRC, Vol. 1 No-3. P.7 and

(ii) Assam Human Rights Commission (Not dated), Commitment to the Child; Guwahati, AHRC, Pp 2-3.

3. (i) Government of India (1998), The Employment of Children Act, 1938 (Bare Act); Allahabad, Law Publishers, (India) Pvt. Ltd. Sections 3 and 4.

(ii) Also, Letter from Section Officer, Supreme Court of India, New Delhi to the Chief Secretary, Government of Assam, Letter No. D. No. 157/86/SC/PIL WRIT, dt. 18th December, 1996.

(iii) Government of Assam (1994), Assam Shops and Establishment Rules, 1976; Rule-48, Form- 'Q', Certificate of Registration.

4. (i) Kula shreshtha, J.C. (1994), *Indian Child Labour*, New Delhi, Uppal Publishing House, Pp. 27-42.

(ii) AHRC, (not dated), *Supreme Court on Child Labour*, Calcutta, AHRC, Pp. 24-25.

(iii) Reddy, Y.S. (1999), *Child Labour: Some issues and solutions*, edited by Y.S. Reddy, *Child Labour*, New Delhi, Anmol Publications, Pp 6-10.

(iv) Kumar, B (2000), *Problems of Working Children*, New Delhi, ABH Publishing Corporation, pp. 50-51, 58-59, 67-68 and 90-91.

5. ILO (1992), The World Labour Report, 1992 and Y.S. Reddy edited (1999) *Child Labour*, P.35.

6. *Note:* Professor (Dr.) H. Goswami of Dibrugarh University, holds the view that apart from internl migration from the rest of Indian states, international migration of people from the neighbouring countries into Assam is very significant. Most of such migrants (84.85% in 1991) are from Bangladesh and Pakistan.This has caused higher population growth (23.58%) in Assam than the all India average (23.50%) during1981-91.

7. *Notes*: Late 1950s refers to the average over 1957-58 to 1959-60. Early 1990s refers to the average over 1990-01 to 1993-94.

(i) Parikh, Kirit, S. (edited, 1999), *India Development Report, 1999-2000*, New Delhi, Oxford University Press, Table- 3.2, P.51.

(ii) Economic and Financial Data - India, *Southern Economists*. (15 June, 2000) Vol.40, N-4.

8. Reddy, Y.S. (1999), *Child Labour*, New Delhi *op. cit*, p. 36.

9. UNDP (2000), *Human Development Report*, New Delhi, Oxford University Press, Table - 19, Demographic Trends, pp. 223-226.

10. *Ibid*, p. 170.

11. *Ibid*, p. 31

12. UNICEF (1998) *Convention of the Rights of the Child*, 1989, (Assamese version) Article, 1 and 3, pp. 49-50.

5

Determinants and Dynamics of Child Labour

Scholars subscribe to various models in explaining the determinants and analysing the causes of or forces behind the incidence of child labour of varying degrees across time and/or space.

Models of Child labour Supply

One accepted model of the 20th century explaining the causes of existence of child labour is Becker's *Micro Theory of Fertility* (1960). The model was explained with the help of Hicksian indifference curves, showing that the higher the level of the curve on the indifference map, the higher is the fertility and higher might be the incidence of Child-labour.[1] Becker's Micro Fertility Model on child labour was refined in subsequent period by Blake, Mincer, Easterlin, Namboodiri, Leibenstein and Codwell. Dinesh (1988) strongly supported the Becker's model with quantitative information, according to which child labour is the consequence of larger number of siblings in a family fundamentally caused by high fertility of mother.[2]

Mother's fertility is stated to be high, if it is influenced by parents' motive to have children mainly to satisfy- (a) the Psychic utility and (b) Economic utility.

Economic utility which refers to prospective benefit and/or tangible returns expected from children may be sub-categorised as -

i. income benefits,

ii. work benefit and

iii. security benefit in the old age of parents.

This micro fertility theory of child labour can not be accepted as fully valid. Because, it is found that some nuclear or small families too send their children to labour market which shows that the underlying causes of child labour supply are not necessarily the higher level of fertility of mother. It is the result of a macro-situation and not of a micro-situation in a family. A study on French speaking African countries observes that poor economic and social environment in which families live makes them to send their children to work inevitable.[3]

Another popular theory of child labour is the extreme poverty with high or low fertility.[4] Under such a theory it is argued that the phenomenon of child labour practices is very much determined by the degree of parents' poverty and the survival strategies of parents.[5] Thus, poverty has been identified as one of the main determinants of the child labour supply. For, in a non-poor high wage society parents do not send their children to work.[6]

Surveys conducted by the ILO and the World Bank (WB) also confirm that child labour work participation rate is of highest level in the poorest region and countries. The child work participation rate or incidence of child labour is defined as the ratio of number of (main plus marginal) child workers aged 5 to 14 or 18 to the number of children in the population in that age group. Accordingly, child labour participation rate is found to be as high as 32.9 per cent in Eastern Africa, in Western Africa it is 24.2 per cent, in East Asia 20 per cent, in South Asia 14 per cent, in South America 12.8 per cent and in South East Asia 11.1 per cent.[7]

In India, one study finds the work participation rate of child labour is declining from 7.6 per cent in 1981 to 5.4 per cent in 1991. It finds that work participation of Children in rural areas is higher (9.0% in 1981 and 6.4% in 1991) than in Urban areas (2.7% in 1981 and 2.0% in 1991) and that the work participation rate in rural areas is declining faster.[8]

Another study also shows, work participation rates of both male and female children in India have been declining from 14.6

per cent and 10.6 in 1961 to 9.9 per cent and 4.0 per cent in 1971, to 5.2 per cent and 3.4 per cent in 1991, respectively.[9]

These studies have shown poverty, either in the form of low per capita income, illiteracy, ignorance and others, as main determinants of work participation of children.

In the present study the trend of child work participation for India has been found to be of 'U' shape due to similar reasons. For, the work-participation rate of children has declined from 12.6 per cent in 1961 to 7.1 per cent in 1971, and then it increases to 7.6 per cent in 1981, to 11.4 per cent in 1991, to 14.4 per cent in 2001. It is expected to go up to 20.5 per cent in 2015. (Table-2.3).

A counter view holds that poverty as the reason for supply of child labour is partly true.[10] ILO is also of the opinion that poverty combined with traditions, compel the children to follow the foot-steps of their parents.[11] But poverty, it is admitted that, is not the only reason for the existence of child labour.[12] In studies across the Inidan states, no correlation has been found between incidence of poverty and incidence of child labour.[13]

Sociologists consider school drop-outs as the important reason for existence of child labour. But, as regards the reason of school drop-outs, there is a difference of opinion between these who argue poverty as the paramount reason and those who attribute the school drop-out rate to the character of school.

According to the National Council of Educational Research & Training (NCERT), New Delhi and some scholars, the inability of the school system to retain children who have enrolled in the primary level education-the "Push-out" has been the single greatest reason responsible for the existence of child labour.[14] Thus, poverty can not always be argued to be the paramount reason of school drop-outs and supply of child labour. It is (poverty) simply a classical defence offered by the apologists till date.[15]

To some educationists the child labour problem is most related to the issue of "Push-out", not to school drop-outs. For another, the more important is that in many cases parents do not know what to do with children once they reach the age of six or eight years or so, primarily due to chronic shortage of primary school facilities.[16] With 1.9 per cent increasing rate of population per year on an average about 48,000 additional children are being added per day in a country like India, since 1990, of whom nearly 44000 survive till the school going age of 6 (six). So, if we plan for a class with 36 students, India needs to construct more schools, atleast 1222 class rooms per day for the accommodation of additional number of school going children added every day. Besides, whereas, even rich parents find it difficult to admit their children to school, it is hypocritical to suggest and impossible to have compulsory primary education for all children in 5-14 age group.[17]

A scholar, Iftikar Ahmed has concluded after a quantitative cross-country empirical study that child labour is basically associated with inequality in society but not with poverty.[18] For, among the seven determinants of child labour, poverty has been found to be ranked last in terms of its explanatory power. Both inequality and poverty in the society have been currently found to be the consequences of capability deprivation - deprivation from quality of being able to do something. And hence, the latter is a more responsible variable for the existence and continuum supply of child labour.[19]

D.P. Choudhury theorises that the phenomenon of child labour - both the incidence of child labour and its occupational pattern, undergoes major transformation in the process of structural changes of the economy caused basically by the complex process of economic growth.

Based on historical evidence of the Western Europe, it has been stated that at the initial phase of industrialisation child labour practices do appear, decline with the spread of industrialisation. In the second phase of industrial development, with the increase in investment per worker, rise in labour productivity and change in structure of the economy, demand for child labour decreases. Spread of schooling and the introduction of compulsory education drastically reduce the supply of child labour.[20] From the economic indicators and child labour statistics of some Asian countries it has also been hypothesised that demand for child labour is affected by technological change, while supply of child labour is influenced by demographic transition. However, the social and political climate, legislations and policy shift of the government have enormous role to play in controlling the size, demand and supply of child labour, either positively or negatively.

It is observed that in spite of such commonality of reasons for the existence of child labour, the incidence of child labour, its degree and intensity vary enormously across time, households, region or country.

Thus, the existence of child labour in a space or time can be expressed in a multi-variate founctional form indicating its main determinants as independent (but they have been observed to be reinforcing) variables.

To put it -

$$mCL = \alpha(Df, Ef, Sf, gpl, Agsy, R)$$

or

$$mCL = \beta + \alpha\,(Df + Ef + Sf + gpl + Agsy + R)$$

Where, mCL = Magnitude of Child labour in existence;

Df = Demographic factors, such as, fertility of mother (Fm), migration (Mg), and Death Rate (Dr);

Ef = Economic factor covers family poverty (Pv), Backward Agricultural practices (Agril), Wage rate of Child labourers (Wr), Transport & Communication, Commercial and industrial development level.

Sf = Social factor includes illiteracy, Parents' Perception to child labour (PPCL), level of Urbanisation, Social & Family traditions (Tdns)

Gpl. = Government Policy covers policies related to child labour administration, affecting and/or reducing the demand for and supply of child labourers. It also includes, govt. legislations and the functionaries controlling, governing and regulating the child labour affairs.

Agril sys = It stands for the agricultural system prevalent in the society;

R = It stands for all the residual factors not covered in the function.

Reasons for Existence of Child labour in Assam

The factors conducive to the existence or continuation of child labour are prevalent in Assam. But, scholars often differ in sorting out and ranking them. Based on field observation, the socio-economic and legal matrixes of child labour in the state have been outlined below.

A. Economic Factors:

In a poor country like India, economic factors such as family poverty, backward agricultural practices, low wage rate, necessity of supplementing the family income for subsistence etc. are considered as the major determinants for the existence of child labour practices.

(i) Poverty:

Poverty, both in terms of lower income and capability deprivation, is a common characteristic in Assam. A considerable proportion of rural population of the state live in poverty. NSSO estimates 20.5 per cent rural population of the state as poor, 67.9 per cent as less well-off and only 11.6 per cent as better off.

About 60.3 per cent (30,41,666 Nos.) land holdings in the state are below one hector.[21] Thus, in rural Assam, such small land owners hire out their holdings. Landless agricultural labourers too sell out their labour for livelihood. Both these classes of people employ themselves in agricultural sector under the big land owners and be at their mercy for wages due to their weak bargaining position. Such agri-labour class continue to live in poverty with a falling standard of life. Due to increasing family poverty their children never attend the school or they drop out at the early stage. The parents take such children to work together or put them into work in some-one else's household or farm so as to earn some extra wage as well as get rid of the responsibility of maintaining the child by themselves. Most of such children have to work not in presence of their parents or close relative, and their masters try to get work done far in excess of their capacity. Thus for the poor families children become both asset and liabilities to the parents. Impoverishment of family life, either due to personal incapability, family disaster, natural calamity or exploitative market operations has been observed to be the major cause which has resulted in perpetuation of child labour practices in the state.

The updated rural poverty line (RPL) for 1995 sets the monthly per capita income (MPCI) at Rs. 228.9, which has been supposed to satisfy the minimum calorie requirement of 2400 per capita per day (Pcpd) in rural India. According to this measure, as shown in Table -5.1, only 32.0 per cent h/hs out of 187 child labour supplying sample h/hs are below the poverty line. This measure of 1995 is long debated. For, this estimate assumes that the consumption basket of the base year (1973-74) does not change and the head count ratio (HCR) correctly identifies the caloric deficient group. A study observes, the true cost of adequate calories in 1993-94 was found to be not Rs. 206 but Rs. 320 (for rural poverty line) and by the turn of 2001 A.D. it would be much more than that.[22]

Measuring in terms of NSSO's 50th round of poverty estimates in 1993-94 it is found that from 77.0 per cent to 97.3 per cent h/hs out of 187 are below the poverty line (Table-5.1). And hence, they are the suppliers of child labourers.[23]

Taking an income of one dollar a day or its nominal exchange rate Rs. 40, a World Bank measure of poverty, it is found that all these 187 child labour supplying sample h/hs are below poverty line.

For confirmation of this fact, these sample h/hs have been re-examined in terms of minimum food requirements, calorie available from such items, true cost of these (in Rs) and the income required Pcpd in Table - 5.2.

It is observed that to acquire various food items available in rural area giving the subsistence calorie requirement (of 2100), a rural family of five members (2 adult + 3 children) needs a monthly

Table–5.1
Distribution of Child labour Supplying House holds According to their Per Capita Per Month Income (Pcpmi) Level.

Survey area	No. of h/hs Having Monthly Percapita income. (MPCI) in between.					Total h/hs
	Rs 25-199	Rs 200-229*	Rs 230-379	Rs 380-539**	Rs 640-629	
Amguri	4	5	12	7	x	28
Nazira	10	-	21	5	x	36
Sunari	16	-	7	1	x	24
Sivasagar-Gorisagar	9	2	11	4	2	28
Nitai-Demow	13	2	32	21	3	71
Total	52	9	83	38	5	187
% to total of 187	27.81	4.81	44.38	20.33	2.67	100.00
% Accumulated	27.81	32.62	77.00	97.33	100.00	

Source:- Primary field survey data

* Up dated Rural Poverty line for India for 1995, (Rs 228.9 Rounded off).

** Range of poverty line Rs. 380 and Rs 540 taken by NSSO in its 55th round of household survey in 1999-2000 (on 30/7 days recall).

*** Our estimates of Income Required Pcpm is Rs 750 for the minimum of 2100 Calorie per capita per day (Pcpd) Requirements. This minimum Calore Requirement as prescribed by J. Mehta and S. Venkat Raman in 2000 A.D. is 1968 Calories Pcpd.

Table–5.2
Average Requirements for Subsistence living by a Rural Family of 5 (2 adult + 3 children) Members

	Item	Period/ time	Weight of items	Pcpd calories avalilable	Pcpd* True cost in Rs.	Cost of a Rural family of 5 members per month in Rs
1	Coarse Rice	1 day	400gm	1320	4.00	600.00
2	Tea	1 day	2 cups	85	4.00	600.00
3	Biscuit/other	1 day	25 gm	95	3.00	450.00
4	Dal	1 day	25 gm	145	0.75	112.50
5	Lemon	1 day	1 No.	30	1.00	150.00
6	Cabbage	1 day	100 gm	18	2.00	300.00
7	Carrot	1 day	100 gm	26	4.00	600.00
8	Onion	1 day	100 gm	22	2.00	300.00
9	Potato	1 day	100 gm	85	1.00	150.00
10	Tomato	1 day	100 gm	18	2.00	300.00
11	M.Oil	1 day	25 gm	260	1.25	187.50
	Total	1 day		2104	25	3750

* At current market price in a rural market of Sivasagar district, November,2002.

income ranging from Rs. 3,000 to Rs. 4,000 at current prices. All the 187 sample h/hs supplying 245 child labourers are much below this minimum income range. Hence it is not surprising that they had to hire out their wards for supplementing the income.

It has also been found that certain landless poor families in rural areas, being myopic of urban life have migrated to urban centers. The jobless parents of such vagabond families being incapacitated by malnutrition, illness or being non-adoptive or incapable of keeping body and soul together approach certain employers and solicit for job for their young children in order to supplement the family income and survival of the child itself. The callous exploitation of helpless child labourers thus starts in urban private establishments.

The hotels, dhabas and some commercial establishments have now been experiencing heap with such migrant child labourers from rural areas of the state. *(Child labourers in urban centers in Assam coming from outside of the state is also significant). Employment of children as house servant in urban-households have added only to the abuse of child labourers. So, in most of the states in India including Assam, family poverty has come to be identified as the major determinant of child labour.

In some cases parents put their children to work as apprentice to acquire the skill in certain technical works like motor-mechanic, carpentry etc. Out of 245 sample child labourers 4 (1.6%) are found to be in such apprentice job.

Analysing the reasons of school-drop-outs it has been found that poverty alone compels 74 (30.2%) sample child labourers out of 245 to drop schooling halfway. Similarly, poverty kept another 72 of them (29.3%) out of school (Table-5.3).

As seen in Table - 5.4, poverty alone compels 96.7 per cent children (232 out of 245 Nos.) to share the adult work, to help the parents in making the household a relatively viable unit of production and to supplement the parents' income. Thus, children denied of schooling and education due to family poverty are the dominant forces behind the continuous generation and expanding child labour force in the state.

Table–5.3

Reasons of School Dropout of the Child labourers in the Respondent Families (in Numbers)

	Amguri	Nazira	Sonari	Sivasagar & Gaurisagar	Nitai-Demow	Total % to Total
I. Prematured death of father/mother & very bad economic conditon	4	6	2	5	-	17 (6.94)
II. Worst economic condition/Family poverty	-	12	4	5	53	74 (30.20)
III. School dropped as per advice of the parents to earn livelihood for the family/ to support the family income	7	9	0	10	5	31 (12.65)
IV. To learn a profession to earn the family bred	9	0	0	0	6	15 (6.12)
V. Not interested/ refused to go to school	2	0	0	2	4	8 (3.26)
VI. Failure in examinations	3	0	0	0	2	5 (2.04)
VII. To earn livlihood at the death of father (& Family poverty)	6	6	2	0	1	15 (6.12)
IX. Father's accident/ illness	3	3	0	0	2	8 (3.28)
X. Have not attended the school due to family poverty	7	0	20	15	30	72 (29.39)
Total	41	36	28	37	103	= 245
% to total Child labourers	(16.73)	(14.69)	(11.43)	(15.10)	(042.05)	-100.00

Sources:- Primary field survey data from Sivasagar District.

Table–5.4
Reasons of Putting the Child into Labour Market

	The Reasons	Amguri	Nazira	Sonari	Sivasagar-Gaurisagar	Nitai-Demow	Total & % to total
i.	Bad economic condition/ livelihood for the maintenance of the family	22	12	24	14	66	138 (56.33)
ii.	The child does not like to attend the school	2	3	0	2	2	9 (3.67)
iii.	Dve to Family poverty/bad economic condition at the death of father and/or mother	14	18	4	8	1	45 (18.37)
iv.	Father's inability to work & poverty	3	3	0	1	5	12 (4.90)
v.	To support the family income-	0	0	0	12	29	41 (16.73)
	Total % to total Child Labourers	41 (16.73)	36 (14.69)	28 (11.43)	37 (15.10)	103 (42.05) →	245 100.00

Source: Primary Field Sruvey Data.

(II) Occupation of the Family & Life Pattern:

Table-5.5 shows that the type of family occupation by and large determines the probability that a family shall be a potential supplier of child labour.

Among the sample h/hs supplying child labour the primary occupation of 34 (18.18%) h/hs is agricultural labour, 32 (17.11%) h/hs marginal farmer, 97 (51.87%) h/hs wage labour, 23 (12.30%) h/hs vegetable vendor. The Table shows that all the h/hs supplying child labour belong to those occupations which are traditionally low-income generating. Hence, they were poor. It is found that agriculture happens to be the occupation of majority households.

(III) Backward Agricultural Practices:

In Assam, 88 per cent population live in rural areas. A large number of them engage in agriculture. The backward agricultural practices followed by such poor farmers and their activities allied to agriculture require more labour to be incorporated in the family work force. The children of minor ages get way into the family labour-force and form an integral part of the household economy in rural areas. Agricultural development may have a good impact but have not reduced the incidence of child labour in the state.

In fact, rapid population growth in rural areas of the state has been observed to be the main dynamic force behind regular fragmentation of land holdings, generation of landless and marginal farmers and inter alia, one of the important matrixes of child labour supply.

(IV) High Wage rate to Child labourers:

B. M. Dinesh finds a positive correlation between the high wages and economic activities of children.[24] By offering relatively high wage rate the employers pirate the child-workers from adult-workers and exploit the former more in terms of work and hours of work. The advent of the multinationals which has accentuated market competition and labour employment has rather prompted child labourers to enter into labour market, for they are paid relatively higher wages.[25] Keeping such points in view, the

Table–5.5
Occupational Pattern of the 187 Child labour Supplying Sample h/hs and the Nos. of Child labourers Supplied

	Occupation of the Child labour Supplying h/hs	Nos of h/hs	% to total	Nos. of Child labour supplied	% to total
	Col. - 1	Col. - 2	Col. - 3	Col. - 4	Col. - 5
i.	Agricultural labour	34	18.18	42	17.14
ii.	Marginal Farmer	32	17.11	42	17.14
iii.	Wage labour	97	51.87	131	53.47
iv.	Pretty traders (carpentary, vegetable vendors etc)	23	12.30	29	11.84
v.	Without Occupation	1	0.54	1	0.41
	Total	187	100.00	245	100.00

Sources: Primary Field Survey Data.

proposed amendment to the "Minimum Wage Act" (1948) by the government of India (GOI) to ensure the child labourers to be paid wages at par with the adult workers would be obviously self defeating.[26] Now children would be sent to proxy their parents in latters' work place.

(V) Improvement in Transport and Communications:

Road length in Assam per 100 sq.kms. has increased from 15 kms in 1961 to 40 kms in 1991 and to 42 kms in 1999. Similarly, railway line per 100 sq.kms has increased from 2.4 kms to 4.7 kms during 1961-1999. The number of vehicles run on the road have also increased from 27.2 thousand in 1965 to over 43.8 thousand in 1971, to 231.5 thousand in 1991, to 294.7 thousand in 1995 and then to 331.6 thousand in 1999. Such developments have linked most of the rural areas with the urban centers of the state. Developments in transport and communications have produced positive effects on agriculture, industry, trade and commerce of the state. Production, productivity and movements of agricultural produce have also increased manifold.[27] Large number of industries both small and medium sized, have been established. The number of small scale industries (SSI) alone have increased from-809 in 1971 to 15,841 in 1993 and to 33,304 in 1997.[28] Several new industrial units and commercial centers have grown up along with the ancillaries in the process of urbanisation. Mobility of people has increased several times. With the improvement of transport and communications many of the Not-School-Attending-Children belonging to poor rural-families have found their way to engage themselves in hotels, shops and commercial establishments in urban centers and in cars, buses, workshops and households. So, after the 1980's appearance of child workers in urban centers has brought the child labour issue to the fore-front.

Till the enactment of the Human Rights Act in 1993, rights of child labour employed in informal sector were very limited. For, common laws regard children as property to their parents, but not as liability to them to educate, provide nutrition, health care and sufficient protein and calorie intake food. So, child poverty and hunger, inter alia, have been observed pushing poor children in rural areas to engage themselves in economic activities in urban centers, where transport and communication developments have played the role of absorbent as well as via-media.[29]

(B) Social factors:

All scholars do not subscribe to the view that the poverty is the root cause of child labour practices. For, in spite of higher poverty level governments of many developing countries have introduced compulsory education in their effort to abolish the child labour practices.[30] For example, South Korea and Taiwan have 90 per cent adult literacy rate, in spite of the developing nature of their economy. Rather it has been identified that child labour is deep rooted in socio-culture and traditions of the society. The mindset of the society has traditionally been such that poor children are born to work with hands, therefore they should be taught how to work; while children of the middle class born to work with minds and they must be taught to learn.[31] Apart from economic compulsion, that is, demand side constraints, most children in rural areas belonging to poorer families and lower stratum of the society join the labour force in their early childhood due to such apathy and strong social views.[32]

Hence, certain social factors determining the child labour practices are being outlined below.

(i) Illiteracy:

Parents illiteracy is positively linked with child labour.[33] In most developed countries like Australia, Canada, U.K. and the USA etc. where the illiteracy is even below 5.0 per cent and the adult illiteracy is not above 1.0 per cent, child labour supply is found to be at its lowest ebb.[34]

In Assam, illiteracy of people is very high. It was 72.6 per cent in 1961, 71.8 per cent in 1971 and 47.0 per cent in 1991. Female illiteracy in the state is much higher (56.9%) than male illiteracy till 1991. It is found that illiterate parents tend to keep their wards off the schools. The parents often argue that they cannot afford the expenses associated with school going, and that spending of five years or 10 years in schooling is a waste of time. So, enrolment ratio of children in 5-14 age group is very low in Assam, only 34.9 per cent in 1961 and 46.7 per cent in 1991 and it is projected to be 47.0 per cent in 2001. Again, a large number of drop-outs at Primary and Secondary stage join in family business and finally add to the dimension of child labour.[35]

(ii) Parents' Perception:

The practice of child labour of the current magnitude in the state is associated not only with the ethos of underdevelopment, with the ethos of Hinduism and Islamism but even with parents' outlook toward the children. In rural areas, parents consider a multitude of male children primarily as an economic asset and as family bread earner. Such attitude of parents and their fertility behaviour purposefully lead to generation of child labour. In the rural areas of Sonari and Nitai- Demow, where agriculture is playing a predominant role, a dismal human development and exclusive concentration of child labourers in agricultural activities (20 or 71.4 per cent and 34 or 33.0 per cent out of 28 and 103, respectively) is seen (Table- 5.5).

Illiterate and ignorant parents have been found to prefer their child to learn a skill or vocation at her/his early childhood so that the child becomes a skilled worker at the age of 15 or so. So, they send their children to work as apprentice in any occupation or train the minor children in family business. Thus, it has been observed that in rural hinterland children are considered as economic asset, and so 'work value' perception governs the parents decision which (factor) ultimately deters them from sending their wards to school. This has led to the assumption that child labour, 'work value' perception of the parents' and the high fertility are the three dimensions of the same thing. As such, logically, parents perceptions are not less significant factor than that of radically unaltered restricted access to and knowledge of pregnancy prevention methods on the parts of the rural poor in determining the magnitude of child labourers in the state as in any other localities in India.[36]

(iii) Urbanisation:

Assam has witnessed tremendous growth in urbanisation, for that matter in the country. Child labour issue is associated, inter alia, with such growth of urban centers. Phenomenal growth of urban centers in Assam from 23 in 1951 to 94 in 1999 and growing employment opportunities in urban informal and unorganised sectors have attracted the wage earners.[37] Not-school-attending children of the poor families in rural Assam (and of urban slums) have caught up that opportunity, quickly.

Higher population growth, rapid growth of personal and commercial vehicles-a demand caused by larger mobility of passengers and freight, and growth of commercial establishments and personal residences have worked as underneath forces to pull the rural children of the poor families to work in servitude in urban centers.[38] Thus, growth in urbanisation has directly contributed in expanding the magnitude of child labourers in the state, particularly in urban centers and has worsened the social polity.

(iv) Family Tradition:

Continuation of family tradition, such as, gold smithy, pottery, carpentry, fishing, cultivation, trading, repairing etc. is a pride and/ or economic compulsion. Certain traditions have been observed in the state continuing mainly due to prevalence of economic poverty,-a decline of which has been claimed to be just spurious in all states of India, including Assam.[39] However intergenerational bonded labour, with children being bonded virtually for life either in agricultural sector or others has not been found during the survey period. But, in most cases traditions, such as fishing, pottery, gold smithy, tannery, butchery, etc. have been found pulling many children to the fold of child labour. Because, parents of the rural poor families consider child work as biological need for sound physical growth of the child and as a social necessity for smoother inter-generational transfer of occupation.[40] The extent of such child-work are found crossing the limit which have compelled many children to drop out their schooling and join the labour force.

(v) Bigger Family size:

Bigger family size has come to be identified both as basic cause of child labour; continuation of child labour practices and determinant of family poverty, rather than it be considered as consequence of child labour practices and poverty determined.

Answer to the quarry of reasons behind a bigger family size are varied such as 'I cannot stop it', 'it is a great gift of God', that 'I was not aware of it till it dried up', that 'my husband not willing to stop it', every child come by an accident', 'when we prepared to limit the family size, by then we have more than five children and the question of going in for family planning or operation (vasectomy) lost its force', etc.

All these are alibi. The continuous procreation of children, as Robert Multhus agrued in his *Essay on Principle of Population* (1798) two centuries before, is the result of passion between the sexes which could never be disregarded by rationalc of benefit of smaller family size.[41] Again, parents who see their children as gift of God, or as advantages, as inheritors of property, as supportive to family income, and/or as security in older ages have been found to have bigger family size.

Parents who enumerate bigger family as an advantage and happy family also found counting the sacrifices associated with it. Though many of such parents are conscious of operation (vasectomy) yet family planning is not done due to feeling of shame and restricted access to it. Thus, then they refer God as an apology for larger family size.

Women of the poorer families do not want to restrict the family size at the initial stage through operation (Vasectomy), for it entails unalterable intervention.[42]

It has also been observed that male child is most preferred over the female one. So, in a hope of a male child the process of procreation continues for several years leading to a bigger family size.

Such poor families having larger number of children fall in the trap of vicious spiral of poverty and disadvantages. For, they cannot afford for schooling of their children, nor can they gainfully employ them in productive work. The illiterate and idle children spoil their valued-life taking part in household works, such as cooking, cleansing, washing, look after younger siblings, animals and also serve the neighbour families without any reward.

In a bid to overcome the economic hardship of the family, the parents put such idle children in family agricultural work or hire them out as agricultural labourer or household servant at very lower wages for direct income generation. Naturally, such poor families (either in rural areas or urban slums) have been observed to have more child labourers who own large number of siblings.[43]

As shown in Table - 5.6 the average family size of 97 or 51.8 per cent sample h/hs out of 187 is within the range of four to six persons; and average family size of 81 or 43.3 per cent sample h/hs is more than seven persons.

As a whole, average family size of the 187 sample h/hs works out to be 6.3 persons. In Amgurie area, it is found to be lower (five), because the family size of this area have been constrained by economic hardship, high mortality of family heads and elders mainly due to undernourishment and unabated use of alcohol. Quite likely, child labourers are rampant among these people.

(vi) Absence of Social Security:

In absence of adequate social security, the children of the poorer families have to take the responsibility of the family members at the event of accidental death of parents.

Table - 5.4 reveals that 45 or 18.4 per cent children are resorting to economic activities due to accident / premature death of their father (or mother) as to maintain their families. 12 or 4.9 per cent children out of 245 sample child labourers are in labour force because their parents are incapable of doing any work on account of their illness.

The state does not have adequate and effective schemes for social security and protection of children in the form of employment guarantee, scholarship for attending the school by the orphans,

Table–5.6
Family Size of the Respondent Families

Area	No. of family according to Family size.					Males, Females, Total Population and Average Family Size in the Respondent Families			
	Less than 4	4-6	7-9	10+	Total No of families	Total Males	Total Females	Total population (M + F)	Average family size
		Nos	Nos	Nos	Nos	Nos	Nos	Nos	Nos
Amguri	-	23	5	-	28	82	75	157	5.607
Nazira	-	24	12	-	36	126	96	222	6.167
Sonari	2	8	14	-	24	92	58	150	6.25
Sivasagar-Gaurisagar	2	13	10	3	28	95	85	180	6.428
Nitai-Demow	5	29	33	4	71	250	216	466	6.563
Total	9	97	74	7	187	645	530	1175	6.283
% to Total	4.81	51.87	39.57	3.75	100	-54.89	-45.11	-100	

Source: (i) As in Table–5.1

against undernourishment and malnutrition of children, for elimination of family poverty, for establishment of orphanage etc. Whatever few child- centred schemes are available, these have not been able to touch the fringe of the family poverty, social insecurity and child labour problems.

So, due to expanding social insecurity under the globalised socio-economic order and competition, inter alia, children belonging to the families in extreme poverty and/or confronting accidental hazardous setback are bound to join in the labour force. Growing selfishness in the society and carelessness for the poor have also been observed to be responsible for the increasing phenomenon of child labour in the state.

C. Administrative Factors

(i) Absence of Compulsory Education:

National Policy on Education (1986) recommended free and compulsory education for all children below 14 years of age. It also emphasised the universal elementary education. Prior to it, for compulsory education provision was made in Indian constitution (Article - 45), for all children up to the age of 14 years. This ideal was to be achieved by 1960.

But in reality, considering the complexity of the child labour problem and impossibility of eradicating the family poverty, government has planned for universal education through incentives, not by compulsion and for amelioration of the working condition of child labourers, not its abolition.

Education has so far been perceived as an instrument of social mobility, social change in desired direction and of having definite impact in reducing the fertility of women.

But, government has not yet been able to make even primary education compulsory. As a result of it and because of massive poverty, children of poorer families get chance to employ themselves at their early ages. Compulsion to educate the children at least up to primary level puts a constraint on parents, make them aware of the value of education and limit the family size. In spite of a good many positive benefits government is hesitating to adopt such rule.

It has been observed that for children of the poorer families in the state school- education lose much of its attraction for various reasons. A few important reasons behind it are that parents' income is not adequate to support their subsequent education, the environment at home is not conducive, the family requires extra income to support the family maintenance, future of the educational career is uncertain, bleak or gloomy and above all, education is not compulsory even up to 14 years of a child.

Thus, mainly the absence of compulsory primary education has been observed to be the important reason, inter alia, behind the prevalence of child labour in the country, including Assam.[44]

It has been observed that in Assam, due to absence of such compulsion over 50 per cent (65% in 1961, 53% in 1991 and 52% in 2001) children of 5-14 age group have remained out of school (Table-3.1). Such Not-School-Attending children have puffed the reservoir of child labourers in the state. Some scholars suggest prohibition of child-employment and compulsory education as viable solutions to child labour problem. But it has been observed that unless the households to which child labourers belong to are supplied with basic necessities, such as, food, shelter, cloth, medicines and free education and education expenditures, child labour practices can hardly be eliminated. Yet, indeed there are many exception to this rule. For, picture and the reasons of child labour varies across household, and across regions and time. ILO, rightly warned, poverty is not the only reason for the existence of child labour.[45]

(ii) Inadequate Nos. of Schools:

In adequate number of schools keeps many children out of enrolment which directly contributes to child labour practices. Professor K.B. Sahay strongly feels that it is not poverty, but the more important reason is the ignorance of the parents who do not know what to do with their children once they are eight years or so. This is primarily due to chronic shortage of primary schools.[46]

In Assam, shortage of Pre and Primary schools is self-evident. There are altogether 30,622 primary and Pre-Primary schools in the state which have enrolled on an average 118 children. The 1991 Census reports that the number of children in the age group of 5-10 who are expected to be in the Pre and Primary schools is 40,33,572. The state thus, requires more than 33,000 Pre and Primary schools of the average enrolment capacity of 120 children. Thus, the state was in short of nearly 3,000 to 4,000 schools in 1991. Most of the Not-School-Attending children found their way in to the labour market being economically emaciated under the new-economic-regime. Thus, for such a reason also, inter alia, during post-1991 period the state has experienced increasing trend of child workers.

The size of Not-School-Attending children and the child population in 5-14 age group has been estimated to be 3.4 lakh and 6.4 lakh, respectively in 2001.[47] With such a magnitude of child population the state is confronting a chronic shortage of schools of over 15,000 of average enrolment capacity of 120 children (Table-3.1).

The state has set a norm to have atleast one Primary school at every one Kilometre distance. In reality, certain rural areas of the state no Primary school is there in a radius of five to seven Kilometres. Though, currently employment of Primary school teachers have been tremendously increased, the number of newly set up Primary schools has not come up in backward rural areas enrolling the home-stayed children.

Besides, despite increasing trend of Not-School-Attending children in the state, Primary and Elementary school teachers have not been asked for taking up annual enrolment drive (AED) of the home-staying idle children in the villages, nor the parents have been put under compulsion for sending their wards to school. So, the situation is aggravating.

(iii) Poor School Environment:

Child labour is not the single mechanism which keeps many children out of school. A critical but common feature observed during the field investigation is that children of poorest families not enrolled or discontinued education or refusing to go to school join the labour market and contribute to the household earnings.

In certain cases parents have reported that the poorness is not an obstruction to sending their children to school. The crucial problem is that, inter alia, deficient of teachers, teachers' apathy in teaching the children, their regular absence in the classes, absence of teacher-student relations are the major stumbling blocks. Added to it that, children do not learn anything in the school, for hardly any teaching is done, and no mental development of children is noticed. Thus, there is waste of resources and human aspirations. In case of girls, in addition to above reasons, their education is considered expensive and useless.

In fact, repulsive school environment with dilapidated school building, broken furniture there in, absence of sincere and loving teachers keep many children out of school and compel many more to drop out half way. A sizeable section of such children find their way to labour market. Table- 5.4 shows, 9 or 3.6 per cent children out of 245 joining in the labour force are only the few among those who do not like to attend school for certain reasons.

D. Legal Factors:

In spite of restrictive labour laws the child labour practice continues unabated. Because, it brings financial benefit to both the employers and the parents of the child labour.

However, the legal provisions restricting the child labour practices are found lop-sided. For, these laws do not cover informal sectors, such as - agriculture, handicrafts, small and cottage industries and household sectors where most children work as house-servant and/or casual wage labourer.[48]

The Factories Act, 1948 permits child-worker in factory if she/he carries a fitness certificate or a token giving reference to the certificate (Section-67). It also permits employment of children below 14 years of age in crafts, if power is not used there.

The Indian Constitution (section 24) allows employment of children below 14 years of age in non-hazardous works.

The Assam Shops and Establishment Act, 1971 sets the minimum age for child-workers at 14 years. The farce of this Act is that, if desired, the government can reduce the minimum age down to four or five years for child-workers.

The Child Labour Act, 1986 specifically mentions about the age limit, hours of work, safe guards for health and work conditions of child-workers. This Act has banned employment of children below 14 years of age in certain occupations, but not in all economic activities in informal sectors. This Act (1986) has not accorded 18 years as minimum age as recommended by ILO in 1973. Nor this Act has repealed the earlier Shops and Establishment Act; and other old Acts. So, there is much scope of employing children of tender ages by overstating their age both by the parents and the employers.

Finally, it has been observed that in the absence of necessary demographic changes, child focused effective public policies and child labour laws, the prevalence of above analysed causes/ variables will be working as dynamic forces due to which the demand for and supply of child labourers in the state would grow with reinforcement and mutual interaction in a spiral type.

Notes and References

1. Becker, G.S. (1960), "An Economic Analysis of Fertility" article in *Demographic and Economic Change in Developed Countries,* edited by National Bureau of Economic Research, Princeton, Princeton University Press.
2. Dinesh, B.M; (1988), *Economic Activities of Children*, Daya Publishing House, Delhi, pp. 4-90.
3. Bonnet, Michel (1993), "Child labour in Africa," *International Labour Review*, vol. 132, No. 3, p. 375.
4. Duraiswamy, M. (1997), "Changes in Child labour over Space and Time in India, 1981-1991", *Indian Journal of Labour Economics*, vol No-40, P. 809.
5. Lieten, G.K. (2000, June 10), "Children, Work and Education - I, General parameters", *Economic & Political Weekly*, p. 2037.
6. Basu, K and P. Hoang Van (1998), "Economics of Child Labour", *AmericanEconomic Review*, vol. 88. No.3.

7. Lieten, G.K. (2000, June 10), *op. cit*, p. 2037.

8. Duraiswamy, M. (1997), "Changes in Child labour over Space and Time in India, 1981-1991", *The Indian Journal of Labour Economics*, Vol. 40, p. 813.

9. Chaudhury, D.P. (1997), "A Policy Perspective on Child labour in India with pervasive Gender and Urban Bias in School Education", *Indian Journal of Labour Economics*, Vol. 43, No. 4, p. 795.

10. Sahay, K.B. (n.d), Child labour; where Schooling is not available; (article) in *Statesman*. Note. He holds the view that non-availability of school is the root cause of child labour.

11. ILO, (1996) *Child labour: Targeting the Intolerable, Report - VI*, Part-1, P.18.

12. ILO, (1992), *Child labour in Tanzania*, pp. 16-17. Note:- Liaberalisation and foreign debt trap have been found equally responsible for child labour.

13. IGIDR (1999), *India Development Report, 1999-2000*. Oxford University Press, New Delhi, p. 65.

14. Weiner M. (1991) *The Child and the State in India*; Oxford University Press, Calcutta, pp. 68-71.

15. Basu, K. and P. Hoang Van (1998), "Economics of Child labour", *AmericanEconomic Review*, Vol. 88, No. 3.

16. Sahay, K.B., *op. cit.*

17. Hazra, A.K. (1997), "Child labour: Some Socio-Economic Reflections", Conference of the Indian Society of Labour Economics.

18. Ahmed, Iftikar (1999), "Getting Rid of Child labour", *Economic and Political Weekly*, vol. 34, No. 27 pp. 1815-22.

19. Foster, J.E. and Sen, A. (1998), *On Economic Inequality*, Oxford University Press, Delhi, pp. 209-211.

20. Chaudhury, D.P. (1996), A Dynamic Profile of Child Labour in India, 1951-1991, ILO, New Delhi, P. 58.

21. Government of Assam, (1996-97), *Economic Survey of Assam, 1996-97*, appendix, Table - IX, Reproduced from *Agricultural Census, 1990-91*.

22. IGIDR (2000) *India Development Report, 1999-2000*. New Delhi, Oxford University Press. (Kirit S. Parikh edited). p. 55.

23. Jones, R.P. and Sen, K (2001). "On India's Poverty Puzzles and Statistics of Poverty", *EPW*, Vol. 36, No.-3 January, 20-26, p. 212.

24. Dinesh, B.M. (1988), *Economic Activities of Children, Bombay*, Daya Publishing House, p. 31.

25. Raj, Krishna (March, 2001), "Improving Labour Standard," *EPW*, Mumbai EPW Research Foundation, Vol. 36, No. 12, p. 980.

26. Bezboruah, D.N. (ed) 1st July, 1993, "Child labour Employers Meet on Friday: Pressure on India to Eliminate Child Labour." *The Sentinel*, Guwahati, p. 7.

27. Medhi, S.B. (1975), *Transport System and Economic Development in Assam, Guwahati*, Publication Board, Assam, pp. 103-104 and 184.

28. Directorate of Economics & Statistics (1999), *Statistical Hand Book of Assam*, Guwahati. Government of Assam, p. 117.

29. Chaudhuri, D.P. (2000), Basic Human Rights, Core labour Standards and Relative Educational Deprivation of Youth in India, *Indian Journal of Labour Economics*, Vol. 43, No. 1. p. 48.

30. Singh, S.P., (1997), Child Labour: The Malady and Remedy, *Yojona*, Delhi, July, Pp. 20-21.

31. Weiner, M. (1996), Child Labour in India: Putting Compulsory Primary Education of the Political Agenda; *EPW*, Vol. 31, No. 45, pp. 3007-3014.

32. Singh, S.P. (1999), Elimination of Child Labour from India, (Y.S. Reddy edited), Child labour, New Delhi, Anmol Publications Pvt. Ltd. p. 96.

33. Dinesh, B.M. (1988), Economic Activities of Children, op. cit. p. 27.

34. UNDP (2000), *Human Development Report, 2000*, Delhi, Oxford University Press, p. 157.

35. Note: A study in Faizabad district in U.P. also reveals similar Results. - Lieten, G.K. (2000), Children, Work and Education - II, *EPW*, June 17, p. 2172.

36. IAMR (1998), Child Labour in Informal Sector, New Delhi, Institute of Applied Man power Research, P. 1. and . Dinesh, B. M, (1988), *op. cit*, p. 21.

37. Directorate of Economics & Statistics (1999), Statistical Hand Book of Assam, Guwahati, GOA, Table - 1.04, P. 10.

38. IGIDR (2000), Op. cit, P. 99.

39. Suryanarayana, M.H. (2000), How Real is the Secular Decline in Rural Poverty?, *EPW*, Vol. 35, No. 25, p. 2137.

40. Bonnet, M (1993), Child labour in Africa, *International Labour Review*, Vol. 132, No. 3, pp. 371-389.

41. Lieten, G.K. (2000), *EPW*, *op. cit.*, Vol. 35, No. 25 June 17, p. 2173.

42. Note:- Whereas % of rural population in Assam in 1991 figures at 88.9 per cent (91.0% in 1971) as per Census data. The main occupation

of these people is agriculture. So, Child labour is prevalent in rural sector mainly in agriculture. - *Ibid*, p. 2177 and Directorate of Census operation, Census of India, 1991 (Assam) series 4, p. 36.

43. Konar, D.N. (2001) "Economics of Child labour and its Relevance in Indian Economy" *Economic Affairs*, Calcutta, (editor H.N.Roy,) Vol. 46. QR-1. pp. 34 and 36.

44. *Ibid.*, Vol. 46, No. 1, January, P.36.

45. ILO, *Children at Work*, ILO. Geneva.

46. Sahay, K.B. (n.d.), "Child labour: Where Schooling is not available," *Statesman*.

47. Note:- (i) Due to non-availability of school and partly for other reasons, the Not-School-Attending children (5-10) of Assam is estimated to be 24,76,548 in 1991 census. Whereas, the magnitude of School-Attending children (in 5-10 age group) is only 15,57,024 out of 40, 33, 572. - Census of India, series-4 (Assam Part), Table C-4, P. 426.

    Note:- (ii) In 2001 A.D. 3429 thousand children (5-14) has been estimated to remain outside the peel of schooling out of 6470 thousand children in 5-14 age group. See Chapter - IV, Table 4.1

48. Different Relevant Acts.

Annexure–5.A
Development Indicators of the North East India

	NES	Population Density, (2001)	PCI (Rs.) 1993-94	Fertiliser use per Hector of Land 1990-91	% of SSI to all India (in 1987)	Per Capita Consunption of Electricity (Kw) 1991	Length of Rail Route per 100 Sq. km. in Kms in 1996	Length of Road per 100 Sq.km. in Kms in 1996
1	Arunachal Pradesh	13 (10)	Rs. 7.9(000)	— (Kg.)	0.01	80	0.001	8.9
2	Assam	340(286)	5.5	10.5	2.23	70	3.14	87.8
3	Manipur	107(82)	5.3	72	0.06	90	0.005	30.3
4	Meghalaya	103(79)	5.8	13	0.07	111	NA	34.9
5	Mizoram	42(33)	7.5	—	—	79	0.007	17.6
6	Nagaland	120(73)	6.6	4.5	0.008	76	0.46	53.1
7	Tripura	304(263)	4.2	20	0.35	50	0.43	124.1
8	Sikkim	76(57)	NA	—	—	—	NA	NA
9	NE Average	148.9	6.1	24	3.28	79	0.77	45.69
10	All India Average	324	7.2	72.4	100.00 (158,260)	290	4.96	227.26

Note: * Total population in the NER in 2001 stands at 390, 35,582 persons, land area is 262, 179 sq.km. including that of Sikkim. Population of Sikkim in 2001 stands to be 540,493 with a land area of 7,096 sq.kms.

** Figures in brackets are the population density in 1991.

Sources: (i) Statistical Hand Book of Assam, 1999.

(ii) P. K. Dhar, The Economy of Assam, Including the Economy of North East India.

(iii) Southern Economist, vol.-40, No.-4, p. 27.

6

Working Conditions of Child Labourers

Children being the future citizen and the repository of all hopes, they deserve special care and attention of the society and need protection of their basic human rights. For, sustainable human development and human rights are inextricably linked. The Human Development Report (2000) has upheld the view that for human development, (economic upliftment and social change etc.) safeguard of the basic human rights is a must.[1]

Among the 16 types of human rights listed in various documents, the basic human rights relating to children are the following[2] -

(i) free and compulsory education to all children;

(ii) no discrimination against children;

(iii) in all matters, the best interests of the children shall be the primary concern;

(iv) the right of the child to life, survival and development shall be ensured;

(v) prohibition of employment of children of school going age;

(vi) ensuring children's freedom from hunger and malnutrition; and

(vii) freedom from cruel, inhuman or other degrading treatment.

The American support for a trade linked labour clause enforced by penalties and sanctions as part of the WTO's activities during

Mr. Clinton administration has brought a new lease of life to the ILO. Unfair labour practices, which might give countries unfair trade advantage have been the subject of close attention of the ILO from the 90's of the 20th century. For that matter, abolition of child labour, freedom of labourers from any discrimination and forced labour have been the ILO's commitment and the fundamentals of the set of core labour standard' (CLS).[3]

India, being a member nation of the ILO, WTO and an acceptor of the United Nations Development Programme (UNDP) has to ensure the 'human rights' (HR)[4] and the children rights to all children (CRC, 1989)[5] and should strictly observe the CLSs. A deviation from the accepted international conventions, core and national labour standard (NLS) and failure to ensure basic rights to children could be an exposure of worst form of child labour practices.

Keeping this in view, working conditions of child laboourers in the state have been examined in terms of the following-

(i) relationship of the child labourer with the employer;

(ii) living and working conditions, working hours, leisure, leave and holidays enjoyed;

(iii) social security and social benefits obtained;

(iv) job satisfaction and the causes of dissatisfaction, if any.

Relationship with the Employer:

As regards the relationship between the child labourers and their employers as shown in Table- 6.1, the behaviour of the employers in case of 70 per cent or 152 child labourers out of 215 sample wage employed and unpaid child labourers has been reported as kind. The employers of 43 or 20 per cent of such child labourers have been stated to be indifferent and of 4 per cent or 10 have been harsh or cruel to the child employees. Moreover, Table-6.8 also reflects that 54.6 per cent or 134 of the wage employed, unpaid and self employed sample child labourers, expressed satisfaction at their prevailing living and working

Table–6.1

Employer's Behaviour to the Child-labourers as Reported by the Parents/Child-Workers

Type of Child labour	Behaviour of the Employer	Total	Kind	Indifferent	Harsh	Harsh & Kind
	Col-1	Col-2	Col-3	Col-4	Col-5	Col-6
i.	Paid Child-labourers	186 (100.00) (86.51)	128 (68.83)	38 (20.43)	10 (5.37)	10 (5.37)
ii.	Un Paid Child-labourers	29 (100.00) (13.49)	24 (82.76)	5 (17.24)	x (0.00)	x (0.00)
	Sub - Total % To Sub- Total	215 (100.00)	152 (70.70)	43 (20.00)	10 (4.65)	10 (4.65)

* Figures in Brackets are the Percentage to Sub-total.

Source:- Primary Field Survey Data.

conditions. Both these findings testify that a better understanding and good relation between the employer and the child labourers exist in Assam. But from close look it is found that the employers pretend to be kind to the child labourers so as to ensure their stay in the job, use them for long hours and get the low and ignoble works done at minimal or no wages. Only a very few employers are found to have shown genuine kindness to their hapless child employees.

A district level labour commissioner of the state opines that had the employers been so kind to child labourers as reported by a majority of the latter, they would have not employed at all the children of tender ages. Instead, he opines, they should have employed adult worker(s) of the family, which the child labourer belongs to. Or they would have co-operated with the state in abolishing child labour practices, sent their child workers to school for education and/or contributed to their rehabilitation and welfare. In reality, the relationship between the child labour employer and the child workers has been found to be like that of a master and the slave. The condition of a child labourer in domestic services is worse than that in servitude.

In fact, the test of relationship between child labour and the child labour employer based on analysis of statistical data collected from verbal reportings of the parents / concerning child labourer does not flash-out the stern reality and the sufferings of the child labourers. For, both the child labourers and their parents are not aware of better living and good working conditions. Many of them are finding themselves better cushioned with what they have- i.e. the existing life pattern, rather than go without employment of young children and meagre income for the family.

Working and Living Conditions

Since child labour in organised and govt. sectors are prohibited by law, child labour in the state is found only in the informal and unorganised sectors, such as in rural households, agriculture, small plantations, commercial establishments, tea shops, hotels, dhabas, construction work, workshops, furniture houses, wielding and motor engineering works etc. Most of these activities are non-hazardous. This is the reason for not having a strong and vibrant anti-child labour movement in the state.

But, child labour engaged in non-hazardous activities in informal and unorganised private and household sectors can be so harmful to the health, safety, educational and moral developments of children that it results in large-scale violation of basic human and children's rights. Out of the 215 paid and unpaid sample child labourers 73.9 per cent or 159 are found working in agriculture and private households. 56.2 per cent or 121 of them have reported working outdoor under sun and shower, so they are susceptible to sickness or disease. They do not get time for recreation or playing. So they are prone to be mentally retarded. 26.5 per cent or 57 of those paid and unpaid child workers are found to have been working in hotels, dhabas, tea-shops and/or private households. Such children work for longer hours and under strict discipline, sometimes in suffocated conditions without rest or leisure. As these children have to perform menial works and dirty deeds, clean utensils, wash clothes regularly, they usually suffer from scabies in hands and feet, ringworm, pneumonia, bronchitis and liver diseases. Such children suffer from anaemia and/or debility and their health breaks at very early ages. Some of them suffer from gonorrhoea, fistulainano, piles, leprosy, T.B, hydrocele etc. due to their abuses and weak health. Child labourers working in the fireplace and cooking sheds in hotels and dhabas are found to be the victims of eczema, anaemia, bronchial asthma and debility. Some of the hotel-boys sleep in the hotel they work-in, in midst of their working and go home at night. Those who stay in the hotel, have to sleep on desk-benches or on the floor of such establishment bare in hot-season, with a rag in winter after the day long-toilsome work. Those who go home during night have to sleep on a cot together with their parents.

Hours of Work, Leisure and Leave

As shown in Table-6.2 out of 215 paid and unpaid sample child labourers 88.8 per cent or 191 have been found to work over seven hours a day. Some others have been found working for 14 hours a day, regularly.

65.1 per cent or 140 child labourers have reported that they are stressed in completing the work assigned and in rendering services for over seven hours a day. It is significant to note that 36.3 per cent or 78 child labourers have to work till night. These two phenomena uphold the evidence of existence and continuation of forced labour in the state in violation of the ILO's Convention (No-29 of 1930) of elimination of forced labour.

Leisure, during the working hours has been observed to be enjoyed, more or less by every child labourer. Out of 215 paid and unpaid children, half an hour rest is found allowed to 18 per cent or 39 child workers, one hour to 73 per cent or 157 and more than one hour rest to 9 per cent or 19 child workers in the midst of workings.

Leaves enjoyed by the sample child labourers have been classified into four types, such as,

(i) festival leave,

(ii) emergency leave

(iii) casual leave and

(iv) weekly holiday leave.

As shown in Table-6.3 altogether 94.8 per cent or 204 child labourers out of 215 have been found allowed either one or another type of leave. No leave is given in case of only 5.1 per cent or 11 Nos. child labourers. Only the casual-wage-paid and unpaid child labourers (26.0% or 56 Nos.) are free to enjoy leave at any time, as they are not paid while on leave. It is indicative of the fact that certain number of children (5.1% or 11 Nos.) have been working as bonded-child labour in the state.

Punishment

Out of 215 paid and unpaid child labourers 43.7 per cent or 94 have the experience of being punished. Of these 7.9 per cent or 17 child labourers have received physical torture and 34.4 per

Table–6.2
Working Condition of Wage-paid, Nominal Paid & Unpaid Child-labourers

Working conditon/ Work place	Total children	Nature of work		Stress on Completion of Work		Minimum Hours of Work				Worked during	
		Dangerous	Danger free	Yes	No	4	5	6	7+	day time	till night
Under open sky	121 (56.28)	3 (2.48)	118 (97.52)	79 (65.29)	42 (34.71)	-	1	8	112	89 (73.55)	32 (26.45)
Under shed, car, in/ outside household work	57 (26.51)	4 (7.02)	53 (92.98)	40 (7017)	17 (29.83)	-	5	4	48	22 (38.60)	35 (61.4)
Unhygienic/dirty/ polluted environment	37 (17.21)	22 (59.46)	15 (40.54)	21 (56.76)	16 (43.24)	-	2	4	31	26 (70.27)	11 (29.73)
Total % to Total	215 100.00	29 (13.49)	186 (86.51)	140 (65.12)	75 (34.88)	Nil –	8 (3.72)	16 (7.44)	191 (88.84)	137 (63.7)	78 (36.3)

* Figures in brackets are the percentage to Sub-total.

Sources:- Primary Field Survey Data.

Table–6.3

Type of Leave Enjoyed by the Paid and Unpaid Child labourers

Type of leave	No. of Child-labourers allowed leave			No. of Child-labour Not allowed to avail leave of the type			No.. of Child-labourers Free to enjoy leave			Sum of the Sub-Total
	Paid-up children	Unpaid children	Total	Paid-up children	Unpaid children	Total	Paid-up children	Unpaid children	Total	
Festival leave	76 (35.35)	7 (3.26)	83 (38.61)	56 (26.05)	20 (9.30)	76 (35.35)	54 (25.11)	2 (0.93)	56 (26.04)	215 (100.00)
Emergency leave	84 (39.07)	8 (3.72)	92 (42.79)	48 (22.33)	19 (8.84)	67 (31.17)	54 (25.11)	2 (0.93)	56 (26.04)	215 (100.00)
Causal leave	73 (39.95)	9 (4.19)	82 (38.14)	59 (27.44)	18 (8.38)	77 (35.82)	54 (25.11)	2 (0.93)	56 (26.04)	215 (100.00)
Weekly Holiday	57 (26.51)	6 (2.79)	63 (29.30)	75 (34.89)	21 (9.77)	96 (44.66)	54 (25.11)	2 (0.93)	56 (26.04)	215 (100.00)
Leave allowed/ Not allowed	125 (58.14)	23 (10.70)	148 (68.84)	7 (3.26)	4 (1.86)	11 (5.12)	54 (25.11)	2 (0.93)	56 (26.04)	215 (100.00)

* Figures in brackets are the percentage to Sub-total.

Sources:- Primary Field Survey Data.

cent or 74 have faced wage cut (Table-6.4), while 3.7 per cent or 8 have faced the withdrawal of facilities. Harsh words or abusive languages are poured in case of defection of any work or fault with the labourers. Such type of physical torture and mental harassment usually demoralise a child, finally push her/him to involve in anti-social works.

However, physical tortures meted out to child labourers in many other states as narrated by Neera Burra in the pages of "Born to work" are observed scanty in Assam. But, the labourious and tiresome-work performed by the child labourers have caused limitless harm to the child labour community in the form of shortening of their longevity, degeneration of health, creation of unskilled-workers, illiteracy and child-poverty. Thus, the vicious spiral of child-poverty and child labour practices comes to prevail generation after generation. The present generation of child labour would beget the future generation of child labour.

Working Condition of Self employed Child labourers:

Self employed child labourers constitute 12.2 per cent or 30 Nos. of the total 245 sample child labourers investigated. They have been found employing themselves in nine (9) diverse type of occupations (Table-6.5). Their occupations/business are entailing varying degrees of risks. Out of 30 self employed young children 33.3 per cent or 10 Nos. have been found engaged in fishing which require least amount of capital and has easy access. Fishing has been observed to be a dangerous occupation if it is undertaken by a self employed child. For, a child may succumb to death by a little fault or by accident. Agriculture and vegetable business have ranked second and third respectively, in terms of risk where 20 per cent or 6 Nos. and 13 per cent or 4 Nos. child labourers respectively, of the sub-total have been found engaged.

Resorting to self employment at early childhood is found arising out of either sickness or early demise of family-head or severe family poverty or for all of these.

Table–6.4
No. of Child labourers Meted out Various Punishment.**

Type of Child labour	Total No. of sample Child labour	No. of Sample child labourers receiving punishment	Physical torture	Wage cut	Abusive language & Harsh behave	Withdrawal facilities
Wage - paid labourers	186	90 (11.86)	17 (7.91)	74 (34.42)	25 (11.63)	7 (3.26)
Un paid labourers	29	4 (1.86)	- (0.00)	- (0.00)	3 (1.39)	1 (0.46)
Sub-total % to sub- total	215 (100.00)	94 (43.72)	17 (7.91)	74 (34.42)	28 (13.02)	8 (3.72)

* Figures in brackets are the percentage to Sub-total, 215

** More than one punishment is meted out to certain children.

Source: Primary Field Survey Data

Table–6.5
Occupations/Business Undertaken by the Self-Employed Children

	Type of Occupations/ Business	No of Child labourers Engaged in	% to Sub-Total
	Col-1	Col-2	Col-3
1.	Fishing	10	33.34
2.	Fish business	3	10.00
3.	Grocery business	2	6.67
4.	Cloth business	1	3.33
5.	Agriculture	6	20.00
6.	Vegetable business	4	13.33
7.	Piggery	1	3.33
8.	Butchery	1	3.33
9.	Furniture work	2	6.67
Total No. of Children engaged in -		30	100.00

Sources: Primary Field Survey data.

Working Hours of Self employed Children:

Compulsion and time limit to work has not been observed in case of self employed children. However, economic needs of the poor family indirectly puts a compulsion on self employed children to resort to strenuous labour. In fact, the responsibility of family maintenance is packed on the back of such children. As such, activity undertaken by a self employed child does not allow to enjoy the childhood and/or prosecute her/his studies upto 14/18 years of age as prescribed in the Indian Constitution (Article-45) and in Universally ratified United Nations' "Convention on the Rights of the Child" (CRC), 1989.[6]

Besides, uncertainity in income earning loom largely before them and it puts heavy mental strain on the psychology of the self employed children. Similar to wage paid and unpaid child-workers, self-employed children (who are still below 15 years) have been found exposed to physical, psychological and/or moral degradation. Many of such self employed children have been observed to be stinty in growth, crooked minded and callous in deeds.

Considering and recognising the harmful effects of non-hazardous child activities on the child labourers, ILO has adopted the "Worst Forms of Child Labour Convention" (No-182) in 1999. This convention (No-182) prohibits procuring, offering or employing a person(s) under 18 years of age in work which by its nature or the circumstances in which it is carried out, is likely to harm the health, safety or moral of the child.[7] So, workings of children in informal/ unorganised sectors or occupations are though more or less non-hazardous but probable to have severe harmful effects on the health, psychology and morals of children necessitate to be banned in the state and for that matter in all parts of the country.

Immediate implementation of this convention would have double edged effect (i) abolition of child labour in informal/ unorganised sectors would be speeded up, and (ii) effective control on population explosion compelling each family to limit the size of siblings could be realised. It is also imperative that together with adoption of and implementation of the UN convention No-182, the minimum age of working for children should necessarily be raised from 14 to 18 years.

Social Security to Child Labourers:

In a judgment, the Supreme Court of India (SCoI) has passed an order in 1996 that the offending employer must be asked to pay compensation of Rs. 20,000 for every child employed in contravention of the provision of the Child Labour Act, 1986. Such amount shall be deposited in Child Labour Rehabilitation- cum-welfare fund (CLR-WF) at district level. The state govt. is also asked to deposit Rs. 5,000 in the same fund for each child employed.[8] Prior to this no social measure, insurance or welfare scheme for child labourers is found in vogue in the state.

But the judgment and the order of the Supreme Court (SCoI) has been found observed most in violation. Because, the order/ judgment carries many loop holes in it. For, the compensation to be paid by the child-employer and the liability on the part of the state arises only when the child is employed in a factory or mine or in any hazardous employment in the organised sector. In so far as non-hazardous jobs are concerned no such obligations are existing; The task of such cases has been left upon the labour inspectors to see that hours of work of such child does not exceed six hours a day and that each child-labourer receives education for two hours a day at the cost of the employer. In fact, the Supreme Court judgment too clearly permits the exploitative child labour practices in a twisted manner. So, child labour has come to be rampant in unorganised and informal sectors of the state for that matter in the country, in spite of the legal (defective?) prohibitions and objections from the academics, NGOs, public and the international agencies.

During field observation, out of 245 sample child labourers investigated, none has been found to be benefited by the explicit and implicit constitutional provisions dealing with the child welfare. Besides, the child welfare granted under the fundamental rights of the Indian constitution has remained a paper work and the will of the wisp for the child labourers.[9]

Other Benefits / Facilities to Child labourers

Table- 6.6 shows that most of the child labourers are deprived of minimum due facilities such as food , clothing, restplace and free-medical treatment during her/his accident or illness. Whatever little facilities extended to a handful of them do not suffice to meet their bare minimal needs. Thus, a section of children badly suffers in malnutrition, lack of health care, education and extreme poverty.

Level and Variation of Wages

The familiar principle laid down in the Minimum Wages Act (1948) for fixing up the minimum wages for a labour in the state and in whole of India is the sum total of -

Table -6.6

Benefits/ Facilities Obtained by the Paid & Unpaid Child labourers.

Particulars of Benefits/Facilities-	Responses		Total No-of sub-total	% to Sub-Total
	Yes	No		
i. Clothing -	45 (20.93)	170 (79.07)	215	(100.00)
ii. Fooding -	55 (25.58)	160 (74.42)	215	(100.00)
iii. Living place/Rest place -	51 (23.72)	164 (76.28)	215	(100.00)
vi. Wages only during treatment/illness	22 (10.23)	193 (89.77)	215	(100.00)
v. Free medical treatment during illness/accident -	57 (26.51)	158 (73.49)	215	(100.00)
vi. Medical aid only (upto Rs 50 only) -	1 (0.47)	214 (99.53)	215	(100.00)
vii. Compensation during accident (equal to wages only)-	2 (0.93)	213 (99.07)	215	(100.00)
viii. Help the family at the time of crises	53 (24.65)	162 (75.35)	215	(100.00)
ix. Nothing -	87 (40.46)	-	-	-

Source: Primary Field Survey Data.

(i) a basic rate of wages, plus

(ii) the cost of living allowances, plus

(iii) the cash value of any concession.

Such a principle has been found to be violated in different categories of child labourers in the state. For example, in case of 11.8 per cent or 29 child labourers wages are not paid except the food and rest place. Such unpaid children have been found to live a slave-life of medieval period. Their lives are at lurk and hinge on the kindness of their masters. Out of 245 sample child labourers 75.9 per cent or 186 child labourers are found employed for different amount of daily wages. Nearly 11 per cent or 20 Nos. of wage paid child labourers are paid below Rs. 10/-, 61.8 per cent or 115 wage paid child labourers (both male and female) have been paid below Rs. 20/-, while 33.8 per cent or 63 Nos. of them are paid in between Rs. 25 and Rs. 40 a day Only 6.7 per cent or 8 Nos. male-child labourers have been found to receive Rs.50 as daily wage which is just equal to existing wage rate for the unskilled adult workers. (Table-6.7).

The daily wages of the paid child labourers have been found varying from Rs. 2 to Rs. 50, and the co-efficient of range is found to be 96.

Average daily income of 40 per cent or 12 Nos. (out of 30) of self employed children has been found varying between Rs. 15 and Rs. 20.50 per cent or 15 children of this category have been earning in between Rs. 25 and Rs. 40 and only 10 per cent or 3 Nos. have been able to earn Rs. 50 a day, (Table- 6.7).

Level of Job Satisfaction:

Satisfaction in an occupation is more or less a psychological phenomenon. It depends upon relative working conditions, ambition, necessity and avenues opened for the person concerned.

During field observation it has been found, as shown in Table-6.8 that out of 245 samples 82 (44.0%) wage paid, 16 (55.1%) unpaid and 13 (43.3%) self employed children expressed their satisfaction at their existing engagements/occupations.

Table–6.7
Daily wages of Paid-Child-labourers & Average Daily income of Self-Employed Children

Daily wage/ Average Daily income	No. of wage-paid Child-labourers		No. of unpaid Child-labourers		No. of self-employed Child-labourers		Total No. of Child-labourers
	Male	Female	Male	Female	Male	Female	
(1)	(2)	(3)	(4)	(5)	(6)	(7)	(8)
Rs NIL	0	0	13	16			29 (11.84)
Rs 2	2	1					3 (1.22)
Upto Rs5	13	4					17 (6.94)
- Rs 10	25 (62.18)	17 (61.19) (61.82)					42 (17.14) (51.84)
- Rs 15	23	5			2 (40.00)		30 (12.24)
- Rs 20	11	14			10		35 (14.29)
- Rs25	7	12			7		26 (10.62)
- Rs 30	21	6 (38.81) (33.87)			4		31 (12.65) (31.83)
- Rs 35	3 (31.09)	7			- (50.00)		10 (4.08)
- Rs 40	6	1			4		11 (4.49)
- Rs 50	8 (6.73)	- (0.00)			3 (100.00)		11 (4.49)
Total	119 (100.00)	67 (100.00)	13	16	30 (100.00)	Nil	245 (100.00)

Note (i) % of wage paid child - labourers (M+F) earning between Rs 2-20/- to total of 245 is 45.71
(ii) % of wage paid child - labourers (M+F) earning between Rs 25-40/- to total of 245 is 25.71
(iii) Co-efficent of Range - (a) for wage paid = 96, for unpaid = Zero and for self- employed=70.

Source: Primary Field Survey Data.

In total, against 45.3 per cent or 111 dissatisfied child workers 54.6 per cent or 134 were of the opinion that they are satisfied. However, they vent up their indignation at their misfortunes and indicated that they have no other go except continuing the present engagement and remain satisfied. In fact, all the child labourers have been observed to be unhappy at the existing state of work and jobs.

Reasons of Dissatisfaction:

The causes of dissatisfaction have been found varying amongst the child labourers in various economic activities. As shown in Table-6.8 and 6.9, out of 82 wage paid child labourers reporting dissatisfaction at the existing engagement/occupation 42.6 per cent or 35 have attributed their cause to low wages, 15.8 per cent or 13 Nos. to ill behaviour of the employer and lower wages, while 13.4 per cent or 11 Nos. to physical tortures.

Amongst the 16 dissatisfied unpaid-child labourers 56.2 per cent or 9 have attributed their reason of dissatisfaction to ill behaviour of their master/employer.

Out of 13 dissatisfied self-employed child workers 43.3 per cent or 6 Nos. have recognised their laborious works which are incompetiable to their age and ability. Heavy work load, family burden and poor income level from the existing occupations are the additional causes of their discontent.

The analysis of reasons of dissatisfaction in three different categories of child labourers working in informal and unorganised sectors of the economy have shown that child labourers in the state have to perform risky, toilsome and unhygienic works. These are similar to worst forms of child labour. Hence, all such child labour activities require immediate ban.

Table–6.8

Number of Child labourers Expressing Job Satisfaction/Dissatisfaction

	Reaction of the Child-labourers	No. of Paid Child-labourers	No. of Unpaid Child-labourers	No. of Self-employed	Total No. of Child-labourers
i.	Satisfied	104 (55.91)	13 (44.83)	17 (56.67)	134 (54.69)
ii.	Not-Satisfied	82 (44.09)	16 (55.17)	13 (43.33)	111 (45.31)
	Total =	186 (100.00)	29 (100.00)	30 (100.00)	245 (100.00)

Table–6.9

Reasons of Dissatisfaction of the Child-labourers

Reasohs of Dissatisfaction	No. of paid Child labours	No. of Unpaid Child labours	No. of Self-employed	Total No. of Child labours
i. Low wages/poor income level	35 (42.68)	-	3	38 (34.23)
ii. Abusive language + low wages	13 (15.85)	9 (56.25)	-	22 (19.82)
iii. Physical torture	11 (13.41)	-	-	11 (9.91)
iv. Unhygienic condition + low wages + abusive languages	8	4	-	12 (10.81)
v. Laborious work + injurious for health + unable to work	5	1	6	12 (10.81)
vi. Inadequate facility + abusive languages + physical torture	7	-	-	7 (6.31)
vii. Heavy work load + risky for life	2	1	4	7 (6.31)
ix. Have to per form low & ignoble work	1	1	-	2 (1.80)
Total =	82	16	13	111 (100.00)

Notes and References

1. UNDP (2000), Human Development Report, New Delhi, Oxford University Press, Pp-1-26
2. Notes- The relevant documents in particular are - UNDP Report, 2000, ILO Publications on Convention on Child labour, Universal Declaration of Human Rights (1948), World Declaration (1990), Report of the U.N. Commission on Human Rights (1993), United Nations Convention on Rights of the Child (CRC, 1989), in Rights of the child by UNICEF, in Preamble and constitution of FAO, Indian Child Labour Act., (1986), Indian Constitution, Supreme Court's verdict on Child labour (1996) and *Indian Journal of Labour Economics*, vol- 40, No-1 (2000).
3. Notes :- The core labour standards are - (i) freedom of association & the right to collective bargain, (ii) elimination of forced labour, (iii) equality & absence of all forms of discrimination and (iv) abolition of child labour.
4. Notes :- The universal Declaration of Human Rights adopted by the UNO in 1948 is a document proclaiming the Human Rights, Standard and Norm. It is based on the principles of UN Charter, 1945. At the effort of the specialised agencies of the United Nations, such as, UNICEF, ILO, FAO and the UNDP a High Commissioner of Human Rights was appointed in India in 1993 by the UN and the office of the UN.High Commissioner for human rights was thus created.
5. Notes :- Convention on the Rights of the Child (CRC), was adopted by Govt. of India in 1989 and it entered into force in 1990. It recognises specific effort for protecting and promoting the rights of children.
6. Note : The Convention on the Rights of the Child, (CRC), 1989 seeks to protect the children under the complete age of 18 years, from economic exploitation and from performing any work which may be hazardous or interfere with their education or harmful to their health or physical, mental, spiritual, moral or social development.— ILO(2000), Action Against Child Labour, Geneva, ILO, Pp.76-77. .

7 ILO (2000) Worst Forms of Child Labour Convention, 1999 ; Reproduced in 'Action Against Child Labour' Pp. 95-96, Geneva, ILO.

8 In the Supreme Court of India, Writ Petition No. 465 of 1986, M.C. Mehta V.S. State of Tamilnadu & Other. Judgment, New Delhi-Dt. Dec.10,1996..

9 Note : The Constitution of India; Implicit Provisions, Articles 15 (3), 24, 39 (e) and 45. Implicit Provisions- Articles- 14,23,38,41,42,46,47 and the Fundamental Rights Article No.-15,16,19, 29 and 30 have granted social security, welfare and protection of children's rights in paper only.

7

Abolition of Child Labour

Policy Framework and Action Plan

Views on the issue of child labour have dramatically changed in the last two decades of the 20th century both at national and international levels. All nations of the world have recognised child labour as a challenge to humanity and barrier to long-term sustainable economic development of a nation and have advocated its earliest abolition. So, India too made a commitment in 1992 to implement the ILO's Convention on the Rights of the Child (CRC), 1989 for complete ending of child labour practices as early as possible by attacking the menace directly through special policy measures, without waiting for the eradication of poverty at first.

But in a big country like India having the world's 2nd largest human population (102.7 crore in 2001 AD),[1] democratic system of government and that too at prevailing back-ward socio-economic scenario with 26.1 per cent of human population below poverty line[2] and 34.6 per cent illiteracy rate[3], the practice of child labour cannot be abolished overnight.

Considering such realities and on the basis of the findings of this research study, it has been viewed that the following measures can be implemented with a view to minimising the intensity and magnitude of the menace of child labour at an early date.

Banning of Worst Form of Child labour.

Government through an enactment of law can ban the worst form of child labour in the state and other parts of the country. The

ILO is also categorical in the abolition of this type of child labour. Under worst form of child labour the following types of child labour activity can be added to the existing ones listed by the ILO.

(i) Children in slavery or similar to child servitude, debt bondage, forced and compulsory labour;

(ii) Children trapped in prostitution, used in begging and in agricultural activities other than at parents' home; and in religious institutions.

(iii) Child domestic workers.

The difficulties involved with it is the identification of the worst form of work and the down playing of the magnitude of worst form of child labour in the absence of reliable field data. Depending on the working conditions, physical environment of work, etc one type of child labour may be identified as worst form in one establishment and the same may be identified as the bad form in another establishment. The local NGOs can be entrusted with this work of identification.

Banning of Injurious Occupations for Children:

Under the existing child labour law (The Child Labour Act, 1986), only 7(seven) occupations and 18 process works have been declared as hazardous and employment of child in such works have been prohibited.[4] It appears that the Act has excluded from its list of injurious works a few more child labour activities which may be regarded as injurious to the physical and mental health of the children. Some of such works are the employment of children in: hotels, tea-stalls and dhabas which are unhygienic and polluted, quarries and coal mines which are suffocating and air polluting, construction and demolition of bridges and buildings which are heavy duty works etc. Government can amend the child labour Act, 1986 as to include these works in the list of hazardous works for children.

Banning of Inter-state Migration of Child labour

In India labourers can move freely across the states. As a result of which, large number of children are migrating from one state to the other in search of works. Such long distance migration of children depriving them the love and affection of home for years together is definitely injurious to their mental health. So, the Child Labour Act, 1986 may be amended and such inter-state migration of children below 18 years of age may be banned.

Raising the Age limit of Working Children from the Existing 14 years to 18 years

This would be in consistent with the UN Convention and the age bar accepted in CRC, 1989.

Kautilya, 2100 yers ago advocated that the minimum age of a child labour should not be lower than eight years. Considering the level of modernisation and the progress of civilization, the minimum age of a child labour now should not be less than 18 years.

Launching Vigorous Awareness Campaigns Among the Parents About the Rights of Children to Education, Care, Well being etc. and About the Duties of the Parents Towards their Children

The NGOs can be entrusted with such job.

Gearing up the Educational Measures:

So far, education up to secondary level have been made free but not compulsory and cost free. So, by making education compulsory and cost free up to class x level and reducing the school dropout by modifying the existing teaching-learning evaluation system almost all the children in 5-18 age group could be retained in the educational institutions. This will automatically reduce the magnitude of child labour. In many under-developed countries the cost free education system has been giving good results in increasing the school enrolment.

Compulsion on the part of the parents to educate their wards, at least up to class X level shall indirectly help in limiting the number of siblings. This can also be used as a strategy for population control.

Providing Incentives to School-Teachers for Enhancing School Enrolment:

District authorities and, or other agencies can introduce financial or promotional incentives to teaching staff of Primary and Secondary schools for ensuring 100% or near 100% enrolment of children in their respective catchment villages/ areas and for reducing/ minimising the number of dropouts in their respective schools. Appropriate punishment in the form of pay cuts, withholding promotion and increments, even dismissal, may be meted out to those teachers who fail to increase enrolment or decrease dropouts in their respective schools.

Revamping the National Policy on Child labour and the NAECL

Realising the difficulties of complete abolition of child labour in immediate future the national policy on child labour (1987) was aimed at

(i) improving the working conditions of child labour by reducing the working hours,

(ii) ensuring minimum wages and

(iii) providing facilities to child labourers for health and education.

To fulfil the above aims of the National Policy on Child labour (NPCL), the government of India has constituted an authority known as National Authority of Elimination of Child labour (NAECL) in 1994. This Authority (NAECL) shall look into the activities relating to the welfare of the child workers, such as-

(i) Initiating legal action against the violation of provisions of the Child Labour Acts, regarding working condition, wage rate and health care facilities etc;

(ii) Adoption of development programmes for the child labour and their families, such as, rehabitation of child labourers, poverty alleviation and employment generation to child labour families; and

(iii) Undertake child labour elimination projects in various parts of the country.

All these three types of action plans of the NAECL have so far borne no fruit either in improving the working condition of child labourers or reducing its magnitude. Most of the action plans have so far remained in the 'plan' form rather than in 'action' form.

To activate the action plans of the NAECL the following measures may be suggested:

a. increase of workforce of the NAECL,

b. opening of branches of the NAECL at district level,

c. formation of district level expert committee for advising the district level NAECL in executing the action plans at district level. Such expert committee may include the labour Commissioner of the district, representatives of local NGOs connected with child labour elimination, local MLAs and eminent educationists. Such an advisory body should be purely non-governmental organisation, which may be reconstituted on expiry of stipulated period.

Rich Cheritable Institutions of the country such as. Om Sai Ram Institute, Vivekananda Seva Shram, Bharat Seva Samittee and the big NGOs, such as Eklabya, CREDA, Mukti Ashram, Lions Club etc.may be motivated to open 'Bal Ashram', Home for Under Privileged Children, Orphanage etc. for the rehabilitation of child labour.

Involvement of Panchayat in the Matter of Abolition of Child labour:

In India, a panchayat is a micro administrative and development unit at grass root level of the society. It can do on its own or it can be entrusted with the responsibility of looking into the affairs of rights of a child and abolition of child labour practices. This can be done by adopting the following steps-

a. At first a panchayat can make a household (h/hs) survey for collecting data from each h/h, which had hired out child labour within the panchayat area, about the reasons for hiring out children for wage work and other information. Thus, the panchayat shall prepare a dossier for each child labour hired out by the h/hs within the panchayat area.

b. Next, panchayat should explore the possibilities of providing some sort of employment generating works to the parents of child labourers, so that they can survive without the income of their children. Allotment of government land for farming to such families may also be considered.

c. A Panchayat may be entrusted with the work of withdrawing the child labourers belonging to ailing and/or disabled parents for transferring them to 'Orphanage' or 'Bal Ashram' or 'Home for Underprivileged Children' and provide such ailing and disabled parents with pensions and other social securities.

Encouraging Participation of the NGOs in Abolition of Child labour:

An NGO (Non-Governmental Organisation) is a full time, 'social welfare oriented, non-profit making legal organisation composed of socially concerned and committed professionals. NGOs are fundamentally different in nature from that of VOs (Voluntary Organisations). For, while a VO is of part-time or temporary nature, locally undertaken people's voluntary initiative to satisfy the local needs, an NGO functions on full time basis with professional experts, with its entity of permanent nature, undertakes activities of various types and works.

For participative action for abolition of child labour practices NGOs are observed to be the most suitable organisations. For, the NGOs operate at grass root level, have better flexibility, base their activities on felt needs of the local people.[5]

Secondly, whereas NGOs (also the VOs) are locally formed, as such they are in a good position to remain in close contact with child labourers and their families.

Thirdly, providing basic services, information and facilities to needy people NGOs (and VOs) can directly combat away child labour practices.

In several countries the NGOs are found to achieve reasonable success in combating the child labour system:

The 'Jatio Sramik Legue' (JSL, 1989) and the Bangladesh Rural Advancement Committee (BRAC) of Bangladesh have been working for abolition of child labour and have achieved considerable success in Bangladesh. The former (JSL) provides vocational training for young children who are out of school, while the latter (BRAC) is operating to provide non-formal education facilities to child labourers with active support from the UNICEF.

These NGOs in Bangladesh have generated interests from the parents in bringing their children to participate in vocational training and/or non-formal education for finding better job.

An NGO called "Casa De La Esperanza" (CDLE) has adopted welfare programme for street children in Panama. It provides them first aid, nutrition, the vocational education, sporting and musical facilities and the primary health care and health services through volunteer doctors.

DLG (De Lass Gul), an NGO of Pakistan, has been working for vocational training, literacy promotion and education of poor and disadvantaged children including the school dropouts and out of school children. The main objectives of the DLG are -

a. Withdrawing the children from begging or other street based works,

b. Providing alternative vocational skill and training to children who have been working for one reason or another and to shift them to safer occupation, and

c. Providing relax to the street children who have not been withdrawn because of parents' objections.

These welfare programmes of DLG have considerably reduced the magnitude of child labour in Pakistan.

The CWINC (Child Workers in Nepal Concerned Centre) is

an NGO of the human rights activists of Nepal. It has been working to serve the special needs of younger girls and married women and to abolish the bonded child labour system called - 'Kammaya' prevalent in Nepal. This NGO has also been using the Cheli-Beti Programme (CBP) of the government of Nepal to educate the out of school children, eliminate the child labour and rehabilitate the child victims. "Maity Nepal," another NGO of the country has been carrying out campaign against child trafficking with the help of college students, provides shelter, basic education and vocational training for the girls who are at the risk of selling or have been rescued from prostitution.

An NGO known as "Visayan Forum" of Philippines has been providing out-reach services to the child domestic workers. It has launched a project with IPECL support in 1995 and has been successful in providing welfare services to the domestic child labourers, in generating understanding of the child labour problem by the society and policy makers.

In India several NGOs have been working for child labour abolition. The NGO, "Mukti Ashram" has been working at New Delhi area and has been able to rehabilitate over 1600 children since 1990. This NGO has a link with SACCS (South Asian Coalition Against Child Servitude). The main objective of it is to fight away the bondage. For, most children (6-7 age group) are lured away, kidnapped and taken to workplace, in industry, mine, construction sites, agricultural field etc, hundred miles away from home. Such young children are confined to toil day in, day out without wages or cash. 'Mukti Ashram' has been successful in setting free many of such bondaged child labourers.[6]

The NGO, CREDA (Centre for Rural Education and Development Action) has been struggling from 1982 onward to set free the bonded children in the factories in Mirzapur-Bhadohi carpet manufacturing belt of Uttar Pradesh. With a mission for abolition of child labour, CREDA has met the parents of working children, child labourers, school children, neighbours of child labour owning families, adult weavers, loom owners, panchayat authorities and the carpet manufacturers. Bhadohi and its surrounding areas contribute 80 per cent of India's total carpet production (most of which are exported) and it is the nerve centre of child employment. CREDA has succeeded significantly in reducing the magnitude of child labour in carpet looms of U.P.[7]

Eklabya (1972), an NGO of M.P. has made a gigantic stride in universalising the primary and secondary education. Eklabya has choosen to work through government schools on improving the science education programme, to help make education more dynamic and meaningful and thereby reducing the school drop-out and the primary stock of child labour force.[8]

CINI- Asha and Pratham other two NGOs of India have been working for abolition of child labour in West Bengal and Maharastra states, respectively.

In Assam, the NGO called Gyan-Bigyan Sammittee is faring well in lower Assam which has been stressing on primary education as an alternative of child labour.[9] The NGO, called "Rural Multi-media Publicity and Promotion" with its head quarters at Golaghat has been providing orientation training on prevention of HIV/AIDS among the child workers and to raise awareness against bad-effects of child labour.

The ICCW of Assam branch (Indian Council for Child Welfare), a national voluntary organisation has been adopting welfare programmes for street and destitute children in the state from 1967 onward. Under the welfare programmes ICCW provides non-formal education, recreation facilities, vocational training, supplementary nutrition, health check-up to deprived and disadvantaged street children. With its head-quarters at Guwahati, it runs six street children centers in Kamrup district stationed at (i) Paltan Bazar, (ii) Santipur (Bharalumukh) (iii) Noonmati (Mathgoria), (iv) Aryanagar (Charapbhati), (v) Sivanagar (Hengerabari) and (vi) Bhatpara (Hatigaon). Besides these, the Kamrup District Council for Child Welfare (KDCCW) runs five child labour school (Pohor) in the Guwahati city and providing welfare facilities and non-formal education to them. These have reduced the magnitude of child labour in the city, significantly.

In this analysis we observe that the NGOs (also the VOs) are better positioned and have greater opportunity to educate the children and their parents about the rights of child, child labour issues, etc. The NGOs can popularise the necessity of single or two children norm, make the parents aware of their responsibility toward their wards, ease and increase the access of children to education and promote the quality of primary and secondary education to stop the school dropout.

The NGOs may start up child labour abolition activities participating in the ILOs Programme on Elimination of Child labour (IPECL) by discovering and denouncing the child labour abuses, lobbying and advocating for children's rights, bringing about policy reform, providing direct service to rescue the bonded children and their families and the children in worst form of activities.

The NGOs may provide financial help, guidance and monitoring from time to time to ensure 100 per cent enrolment of children in the primary and secondary stage of education. Thus, the NGOs may become successful in reducing the primary stock of child labour and abolishing the child labour practices.

Involvement of Government Departments:

Example of joint ventures of the government departments and the NGOs in abolition of child labour are plentiful.

In Philippines a Multi-Grade Education Programme (MEP, 1995) was initiated by the Department of Education, Culture and Sports in cooperation with the NGOs and started setting up schools for the poor only. They organise monthly workshops for teachers to sustain their continuing professional development and to wean away the problem of isolation of the teachers.

In Costa-Rica, the Ministry of Public Education has been executing a national programme for child labourers through the local NGOs in coordination with the Ministry of Health Department. The programme is popularly known as PANI (National Children's Patronage) and it covers providing of nutrition & health care and education to street children and child labourers in informal sectors.

Similar steps have been taken in Thailand, Tanzania, Peru, Nepal, Brazil, Uganda, Bolivia, etc. to phase out child labour and to provide viable alternative to such children.

Govt. of India and the state governments may take up such efforts in cooperation with the local NGOs in order to execute the action plans for abolition of child labour in the country.

Activating the Role of Human Rights Commissions :

After the formation of National Human Rights Commission (NHRC) in 1993, like in other states of the country the Assam Human Rights Commission (AHRC) was constituted in March 1996, by the Assam government under the provision of the Protection of Human Rights Act, 1993. The headquarters of the AHRC is at Guwahati. The five members state level Commission headed by a retired chief justice has been functioning with vigour, difficulties and certain limitations. For example, the AHRC has registered 3,457 cases in the last six years of which 700 cases are pending with it. The commission has registered additional 165 cases Suo-motu under section -12 of the Protection of Human Rights (PHR) Act, 1993, on the basis of the News Papers' reports, till 1997.

With due concurrence of the Chief-justice of the Guwahati High Court (GHC), the Commission has specified 12 district session courts in the state to be the Human Rights Courts (HRC) of the respective districts for providing speedy trials of the offences arising out of violation of human rights.

The Commission has been mobilising public opinion against child labour practices through holding seminar, delivering popular lectures, casting T.V. programmes and undertaking project study on the conditions of working children in the state.

Besides, the AHRC in collaboration with the "Law Research Institute for Eastern Region" at Guwahati High Court and Women's Studies Centre (WSC) of Guwahati University with the fund assistance of the UNICEF nas completed two studies on child labour in the state. But, not a child labour related case has still been found filed with the AHRC, or taken up as Suo-motu to date.[10] Thus, growing trend of child labour practices and exploitation of child labour is the phenomenon of largest human rights violation in the state. The NHRC and the state level Commissions, including the AHRC may become pro-active to regulate and minimise the long awaited problem of child labour practices.

Auditing the Child labour Aboliton Works and Financing the Panchayats and the NGOs for Child labour Abolition Projects Through a Single Window:

Auditing the child labour abolition works and the financial accounts of fund utilising organisations such as, NGO, Panchayat and government department etc. by a group of experts from time to time under the control of the NAECL is essential for the success of the schemes of child labour abolition.

The previous system of providing finance from multiple-sources to the organisations working for the abolition of child labour practices requires to be abandoned. Sanction and release of such funds through a single window of NAECL to the deserving and active NGOs, Panchayat, and other agencies is necessary to avoid misuse of funds. Effectiveness of funds made available can be increased if the funds are provided on project basis and/or contract basis to the active organisations.

Information about the amount of money sanctioned or released and its utilisation may be made available in internet system of the "Community Information Centres" (CIC) and in local news papers. Such transparency of information and detail accounts shall bound the resource funding and resource taking organisations to perform the given tasks sincerely, mainly because of public pressure and open social obligations.

Notes and References

1. *Southern Economist,* (June 15,2000) Bangalore.
2. Note: The figure relates to 30 day recall in 1999-2000. - IGIDR (2002), Kirit S.Parikh and R. Radhakrishna edited, India Development Report, Table - 1.1.
3. *Ibid*; computed from Table - 1.3.

4. The Child labour (Prohibition and Regulation) Act, 1986, pp. 4-11.
5. Hembhai, (n.d.) NGO's and Social Change, an unpublished article, (Guwahati) and Chaudhury, Atanu Kumar, (1998), Voluntary Organisations as a Catalyst of Rural Development; paper presented at NEEA conference, Guwahati (1998)
6. ILO (2000), Action Against Child Labour, ILO, Geneva, pp. 65-255.
7. Khan, S.K. (1998), *Children and the Human Rights*, Commonwealth Publishers, New Delhi, pp. 43-44.
8. ILO, (2000). *op. cit.*, pp 50-64.
9. *The Sentinel*, Sept. 23, 2001.
10. Assam Human Rights Commission (1997, 1998, 1999 & 2000) News Letter, Guwahati, AHRC, Vol. No.-1 (1997), No.-2 (1998), No.-3 (1999) and No.-4 (2000 AD).

Bibiliography

Ahmed, Iftikar (1999) and Lieten, G.K. (2002), Children, Work and Education-I, General Parameters; *Economic and Political Weekly*, (EPW), Vol.-35, No.-24.

Assam Human Rights Commission (AHRC), (n.d.), *Commitment to the Child*; Gauhati, AHRC.

AHRC (Not dated), *Supreme Court on Child Labour*, Calcutta.

AHRC (1997, 1998, 1999 and 2000), *Newsletter*, Gauhati, Vol. From No.1 to 4.

Assam Shops and Establishments Act and Rules, (Assam Act XXI of 1974) 4th edition, 1997.

Bakshi, S.R. and Bala, K. (edited, 2000) *Child Welfare and Development*; Deep & Deep Publications, New Delhi.

Basu, K and P. Hoang von (1998), Economics of Child Labour; *American Economic Review*, Vol. 88, No-3

Becker, G.S. (1960), "An Economic Analysis of Fertility" *Demographic & Economic Change in Developed Countries*; edited by National Bureau of Economic Research, Princeton University Press.

Bezboruah, D.N. (edited, 1st july, 1993) Child labour Employers Meet on Friday: Pressure on India to Eliminate Child labour" *The Sentinel*, Gauhati.

Bhar, B.K. (1977), *Hand book of labour Laws*, Academic Publishers, Calcutta.

Bonnet, Michel (1993), Child labour in Africa, *International Labour Review*, Vol. 132, No. 3.

Burra, Neera (1997), *Child Labour in India*, Oxford University Press, Delhi.

Castle, Robert, Chaudhury, D.P. *et. al* (1997), "Labour Classes, The World Trade Organisation and Child labour in India"; *Indian Journal of Labour Economics*, Vol-40. No.-1

Centre for Development Economics (2000), *Public Report on Basic Education in India*, New Delhi, Oxford University Press.

Chaudhury, Atanu Kumar (1998), Voluntary Organisations as a Catalyst of Rural Development, Paper Presented at NEEA Conference, Gauhati, (1998)

Chaudhury, D.P. (1996), *A Dynamic Profile of Child labour in India, 1951-1991,* ILO, New Delhi.

Chaudhury, D.P. (1997), A Policy Perspective on Child labour in India with Pervasive Gender and Urban Bias in School Education, *The Indian Journal of Labour Economics*, Vol. 40, No. 4. Table- 1(a+b).

Chaudhury, D.P. (2000), Basic Human Rights, Labour Standards and Educational Deprivation, *The Indian Journal of Labour Economics*, Vol. 43, No.-1.

Chaudhury, R.K. (1982), *Economic History of Ancient India*, Delhi

Dinesh, B.M. (1988), *Economic Activities of Children*, Daya Publishing House, Delhi.

Directorate of Census Operation, *Census of India, 1991, (Assam) Series-4.*

Directorate of Economics and Statistics (1999), *Statistical Hand Book of Assam*, Gauhati. Govt. of Assam.

Directorate of Economics and Statistics, (GOA), *Economic Survey of Assam, 1996-97*, Appendix Table- IX

Duraiswamy, M. (1997), Change in Child labour Over Space and Time in India, 1981-1991, *The Indian Journal of Labour Economics*, Vol.- 40. No.4.

Foster, J.E. and Sen, A (1998), *On Economic Inequality*; Oxford University Press, Delhi

Government of Assam, Dept. of Personnel (B), Notification No.- ABP/25/97/8 dt. 29th May, 1998, New Rules 26-A, *Employment of Children*, Reproduced by AHRC (1999) in *News Letter*, Gauhati.

Government of India, (1998) *The Employment of Children Act, 1938* (Bare Act) Allahabad, Law Publishers.

Hazra, A.K. (1997), *Child Labour: Some Socio-Economic Reflections*, article Presented in the Conference of the Indian Society of Labour Economics, 1997.

Hembhai, (Not dated), *NGO,s and Social Change*. Gauhati.

IAMR (1998), *Child Labour in Informal Sector*, New Delhi, Institute of Applied Manpower Research.

IGIDR (2000), *India Development Report, 2000*, Delhi Kirit S.Parikh edited.

ILO, (1992), *World Labour Report, 1992.*

ILO, (1992), *Child Labou in Tanzania.*

ILO, (1996) *Child Labour; Targeting the Intolerable, Report- VI*, Part-I Geneva.

ILO, (1997) *Children at Work*, ILO, Geneva.

ILO (2000), *Action Against Child Labour*, Geneva.

ILO (2000), *Worst Forms of Child Labour.*

Kautilya, (Not dated), *Arthashastra*, Asom Prakashan Parishad, Calcutta.

Khanna, S.K. (1998), *Children and The Human Rights*, Commonwealth Publishers, New Delhi.

Konar, D.N. (2001), Economics of Child labour and its Relevance in Indian Economy, in *Economic Affairs*, Calcutta, vol. 46. No.1.

Kulshreshtha, J.C. (1994) *Indian Child Labour*, Uppal Publishing House, New Delhi.

Kumar, B. (2000), *Problems of Working Children*, New Delhi, A.B.H. Publishing Corporation.

Labour Bureau, Ministry of Labour (1994), *Indian Labour Year Book, 1992*, GOI, Delhi.

Letter from Section Officer, Supreme Court of India, New Delhi to the Chief Secretary, Government of Assam, Letter No.-D.No. 157/86/SC/PIL, *WRIT*, dt. 18th December, 1996.

Lieten, G.K. (2000, June 10), Children, Work and Education-I, General Parameters, *Economic and Political Weekly*,

Lieten. G.K. (2000), Children, Work and Education-II, *Economic and Political Weekly*, June - 17, 2000.

Puri, Rakhat (1984), "India has 100 Million Bonded Labourers", *The Hindustan Times*, Sept. 30, 1984.

Raj, Krishna (March, 2001), Improving Labour Standard, *Economic and Political Weekly*, Mumbai, Vol. 36. No.-12.

Ray. Chaudhury, S.C. (1997), *Social, Cultural and Economic History of India: Medieval Age*, Surjeet Publications, Delhi.

Reddy, Y.S. (edited, 1999), *Child Labour*, New Delhi, Anmol Publications.

Sahay, K.B. (n.d.), Child Labour: Where Schooling is not Available, article in *Statesman*.

Saxena, R.C. and Saxena, S.R. (1992), *Labour Problems and Social Welfare*, Prakashan Kendra, Lucknow.

Singh, J.K. (1998), *Labour Economics: Principles, Problems and Practices*, Deep and Deep Publications, New Delhi.

Singh, S.P. (1997) "Child Labour: The Malady and Remedy", *Yojana*, July, 1997

Southern Economists, 15th June; Bangalore, vol. 40. No.-4

Suryanarayana, M.H. (2000), How Real is the Secular Decline in Rural Poverty ? *Economic and Political Weekly*, Vol. 35, No-25.

The Assam Tribune, (2000), 29th December, Gauhati,

The Constitution of India.

The Employment of Children Act, 1938. GOI.

The Indian Journal of Public Administration, (1979), Vol. XXV, No. 3.

The Mehbub Ul-Haq Human Development Centre (2000), *Human Development in South Asia, 2000*, New York, Oxford University Press.

The Sentinel, Sept. 23, 2001.

Tripathy, R.S. (1985), *History of Ancient India*, Motilal Banarsidas, Delhi.

"*UN Convention on the Rights of the Child, 1989* unpublished article by. P. Hazarika.

UNDP (2000), *Human Development Report*, Oxford University Press, Delhi.

UNICEF (1998), *Convention of the Rights of the Child. 1989*, Calcutta.

Vaid, K.N. (1970), *Labour Welfare in India*, Sri Ram Centre For Industrial Relations, New Delhi

Weiner, Myron (1991), *The Child and The State in India*, Oxford University Press.

Weiner, M (1996), Child labour in India: Putting Compulsory Primary Education on the Political Agenda; *Economic and Political weekly*, Mumbai, vol. 31, No. 45

World Bank (2000), *Entering the 21st Century*, World Bank, IBRD, Oxford University Press.

Index